CAREERS IN

CAREERS IN
SOCIAL WORK
Julia Allen

Fourth Edition

KOGAN PAGE
CAREERS
SERIES

First published in 1980, by Anne Page
Second edition 1985
Third edition 1988, by Julia Allen
Fourth edition 1992

Kogan Page Limited
120 Pentonville Road
London N1 9JN

British Library Cataloguing in Publication Data

A CIP record for this book is available from the British Library.

ISBN 0-7494-0805-7

Typeset by DP Photosetting, Aylesbury, Bucks
Printed and bound in Great Britain by
Clays Ltd, St Ives plc

Contents

Part 1

Introduction

This book is intended for those who are thinking that they would like to work with people but do not know what the openings are. I hope it will prove helpful to school- and college-leavers, job changers and those who want to return to work after, perhaps, a longish break. It should be read together with the companion Kogan Page volume *Careers Working with Children and Young People.*

Social work, in the broadest sense of the term, is helping people tackle the problems they face in their daily lives - such things as bad housing, mental or physical handicap, loss of faculties through old age, marital breakdown, alcoholism, conflict with the law, debt, long-term unemployment - and, very often, it involves meeting them on their own ground, in their own homes. Generic social workers - that is, those who have acquired a Certificate of Qualification in Social Work or a Diploma in Social Work (see pp 86-93) - are not the only people who do social work. The prison officer getting a prisoner to accept responsibility for his offence and prepare for life outside, the occupational therapist demonstrating an aid that will enable a wheelchair-bound client to take a bath, the counsellor helping a couple save their marrage, the health visitor teaching a group of teenage mothers about nutrition, the home help acting as a lifeline for a solitary pensioner and the care assistant feeding a severely handicapped child - all these people are doing social work.

If this kind of front-line, person-to-person work is what you want to do, there are plenty of options. You can take a professional training course and acquire a nationally recognised qualification, or start right in and learn on the job. You can specialise in an area that particularly interests you, or do very varied work. You can live in and be on call 24 hours a day, or put in just a few hours a week. You can work in a large institution or in a small informal set-up. You can seek employment with a local authority, the Home Office, a private individual or a voluntary organisation.

Social work calls for maturity and, indeed, there are certain kinds of training which you cannot begin until you are 21 years old, although, of course, maturity is not simply a matter of reaching a certain age. Also, obvious as it may seem, you should not think of going into social work unless you really like people and feel a concern for their welfare. You must be able to suspend judgement and accept people as they are, respecting their aspirations and working with them to improve their social conditions and increase their autonomy. You will need plenty of patience too, as it can be a long slow process building up a relationship with some clients and you may have to pick your way carefully over barriers of class, culture, religion, race and prejudice of all sorts. You will meet set-backs along the way and will often be disappointed at how little you seem able to do.

The social services are stretched, some of them almost to breaking-point; furthermore, the work can be extremely stressful. Unless you manage to remain detached and impartial, to switch off at the end of the day, you will be less efficient in your work and your clients' problems will spill over into your life. A lot of the time you could be working on your own with your clients, but you will be a member of a team so will get plenty of support and you will be able to call on back-up from other professionals.

From time to time the social services receive a lot of media attention; there are stories of negligent or over-zealous social workers, callousness in old people's homes and brutality in prisons. Professional lapses undoubtedly do occur and, disquieting though such stories are, they concern isolated cases. The great majority of those engaged in social work are dedicated, conscientious people who enjoy excellent relations with their clients.

Some 500,000 people have careers in social work and women outnumber men by nearly seven to one. Training programmes and working methods are continually being assessed and updated and there is a trend towards greater professionalism at all levels. Despite the heavy demands placed on local government social service departments, cut-backs in spending suggest that few new posts will be created.

It has been impossible to give a definitive description of any of the jobs featured in this book as no two employers - whether public, private or voluntary sector - are alike. A number of people were kind enough to read different parts of the text and all made suggestions or comments. However, the responsibility for what I have written is mine alone. The case studies are the heart of this book and I am especially grateful to the busy people who found time to be interviewed. The one thing they have in common is their love of their work and the satisfaction they gain from working with and for their clients; it is their words that will give you an idea of what social work is like.

Chapter 1
Preparation for Work

Social work is more a way of life than a job and while you are still at school you should try to gain some first-hand knowledge of the kinds of clients you might meet or the settings you might meet or the settings you might find yourself in, as this will help you discover whether social work is going to be the right career for you. For instance, you could help out at a local youth club in the evenings or at weekends; if you attend a place of worship, you might be able to involve yourself in visiting or providing practical support for elderly or house-bound parishioners.

Youth Training (YT)

Those who leave school at 16 or 17 can apply for a placement on a YT caring skills programme, currently being funded through local Training and Enterprise Councils (TECs). Trainees are paid a weekly allowance and, on successful completion of the programme, receive a certificate. If you join the scheme and then feel you have opted for the wrong programme, you are free to leave at any time, or you can switch to another programme.

On a caring skills programme you will probably be given work experience with children, eg in a nursery, and with old people, eg in an old people's home. Don't be put off by the idea of working with the elderly; many young people quickly find that they can relate to them very well – perhaps you get on better with your grandparents than with your parents – and the old often blossom in the company of the young.

You cannot do social work under YT as there is a minimum age for social workers, and professional qualifications are needed. However, you will come across social workers if you join a caring skills programme, and will be able to see something of the work they do and begin to understand some of the problems faced by various client groups.

Exams

Many of the jobs described in this book can be done only by those with professional qualifications, so look at Part 2 to see what the entry requirements are for any of the university, polytechnic or college courses you might be interested in and choose your GCSE/SCE and/or A level (or equivalent) courses accordingly. Your careers teacher will, of course, be able to advise you on this matter.

Short-term Voluntary Work

A spell of voluntary work in one of the social work spheres can help you decide what kind of course of study or job you might like, and the experience will certainly be useful when you come to apply for a place on a course or for work.

Some voluntary work is completely unpaid and if you were going to do this you would probably have to live at home. Alternatively, you might join a scheme that provided meals and/ or accommodation and, sometimes, a small weekly sum of pocket-money and/or a travel allowance. If you want general information contact your nearest Volunteer Bureau or Citizen's Advice Bureau. A number of organisations, whose names and addresses you will find on pages 109-111, produce factsheets about voluntary work and lists of employers. It is a good idea to arrange your voluntary work through a recognised organisation as you will be given help in making your choice and may get some support while you are on the job.

A volunteer is expected to attend as regularly as a paid employee, so before you apply be very clear in your own mind how much time per day or per week you are prepared to give and for how long. The Wales Council for Voluntary Action lists some useful points in its Information Sheet:

☐ Do you know exactly what is expected of you? Do you like doing a bit of everything or do you prefer doing something specific? Either way, make sure you know what you will be expected to do and that you are happy with it.

☐ Do you know to whom you are responsible, or whom to go to in an emergency?

☐ Do you know enough about the organisation you will be joining - its structure, the names and functions of paid staff, the names and functions of other volunteers? It is quite likely that someone will explain all this when you start; but if not, don't be afraid to ask.

☐ Is there any special clothing requirement, or will you be using any special equipment?

☐ If you are a resident volunteer, do you know what accommodation, meals and pocket-money are provided? Is there a charge?

☐ Is there adequate insurance cover? Are you clear about exactly what you are (and are not) covered for?

☐ What support, if any, can you expect from paid staff? Is there someone available to help you plan your work and to talk through your difficulties?

☐ Is there a support group for volunteers?

☐ Is there any training available?

Community Service Volunteers (CSV)

CSV is the organisation which pioneered the system of paying volunteers pocket-money and providing them with board and lodging while they are doing full-time voluntary jobs. It has its main office in London and local offices in other cities including Birmingham, Glasgow and Cardiff. Each year CSV places over 2,500 volunteers in projects, trying as far as possible to make sure that people were sent to work for which they were suited. It organises its volunteers in two ways: through a central volunteer network, which is the way most volunteers work; and through a number of special schemes to encourage people who might not know about these opportunities. For example, through the Give and Take Scheme people who have spent some time 'in care' become volunteers, and the Young Offenders Programme takes people who have a record of minor offending.

CSV accepts anyone between the ages of 16 and 35 who really wants to do some community service, who is willing to work away from home and who is able to give a minimum of four months to the work. At the present time, placements are for a maximum period of one year. Volunteers need not have prior experience or any educational qualifications. No one is turned down, though sometimes people withdraw their applications after interviews which perhaps have made them realise that they are unsuited to community service. This policy of accepting everyone who wants to become a volunteer makes the interview a very important part of the work of CSV. Through the interview, people's strengths and weaknesses are discovered and discussed, and decisions are made about possible kinds of work. No one is sent out to do work which is likely to make impossible demands on them.

How to Apply

If you want to become a Community Service Volunteer you must write to the London office for an application form (see p 109 for address). This form asks questions about yourself, your interests, abilities and future plans, and requires you to give the names and addresses of two referees. You will then be asked to attend an interview at the CSV office nearest your home. At the interview you must answer all questions honestly, as the main point of the questioning is to find out something about you and fit you into a placement to which you will be well suited and where you will be happy. Remember that nothing will exclude you from community service, not even an episode about which you may be embarrassed like a brush with the police. If, for example you have had a period of psychiatric illness, it might simply mean that there were certain kinds of work which could place too much stress upon you and should be avoided.

As most placements involve living away from home, free accommodation and board are provided. If no accommodation is available on the job, you will be given a weekly food allowance and provided with self-catering facilities. Your travelling expenses to and from the place of work at the beginning and end of your placement will be paid and you will get one week's holiday for every four months you work, again with the return fare to your home paid. You are also paid weekly pocket-money and as a volunteer you do not pay any tax or insurance.

CSV places volunteers in any work which is not commercial, and a lot of this work is with children. There are opportunities to work with the handicapped in homes, hospitals, on educational projects and, occasionally, on a one-to-one basis in their families. Help is given with children in clubs, playschemes and in a youth setting, and CSV cooperates with Juvenile Justice and Youth Training schemes. Finally, however, your placement will depend on what is available at the time you apply.

Advantages

The main advantages are in terms of the experience the work will give you. If you are a school-leaver, a year away from home will make you more mature and able to cope with a job or with further education. If you are older and intend to change your career, you will want to be really sure that you are suited to the new work before embarking on training or a paid job. The sustained nature of CSV work allows you to discover if you can stand the pace, stress and demands of the job. In a very practical sense, you will fulfil the requirements of many training courses for a year's experience, you will make contacts who may be useful in supplying references when you make applications for training courses or jobs, and you may even find yourself a job as you could be asked to stay on as a paid employee at your volunteer placement.

Case Study

Anna is a Community Service Volunteer, spending one year in an inner city area.

I spent one year at further education college after leaving school and got two A levels. Then I got a job in a big commercial office, and I found I wanted the chance to work more closely with people, rather than with paper, but I didn't know in quite what way. I heard about CSV which gives you the opportunity to work in a variety of different settings, so I thought that would be a good way to find out about things which interested me, while doing something useful, I hope, for others. The social workers have made me very welcome, and I've been asked to do things as varied as helping one old man move house, collecting the pension for another who couldn't get out, working with a local community association which wanted to start activities like a mother-and-toddler group, and helping at a lunch club for pensioners, which needs lots of willing, energetic people.

It seems to depend where you are placed as to how much supervision and direction you get - some CSVs seem to be expected to just sort of pick up things to do around the place; others have a quite precise role set out for them. It can seem a bit directionless at first, if you don't know anything about social or community work, but learning on the job like this is a great experience. It's a good way of bridging the gap too, between living at home and living on your own - you get your lodging organised for you and a small expense allowance, and you quickly learn the implications of not having much money to spend.

Chapter 2

Jobs Requiring Few or No Qualifications

There are a number of jobs requiring few or no qualifications which are suitable for people who wish to gain work experience before taking a social work course, for job changers or for mature applicants starting work, say, after bringing up a family. Very often, all you will need is common sense and your employer, and/or those you work with, will show you what to do. Unfortunately, these jobs are usually poorly paid and offer no promotion prospects and there is a danger that some private employers will exploit unqualified staff. Before you accept employment, obtain a written description of your duties, find out to whom you will be directly responsible, and, if you are going to work in an institution, ask to see round it.

Probation Service

There are posts in the probation service for unqualified probation assistants, hostel staff and community service supervisors. Contact your local branch of the probation service whose address will be in the telephone directory. (For details of work in the service see Chapter 5, pp 50-56.)

Residential and Day-care Work

Local authorities and private or voluntary organisations need care staff or care assistants to work in day centres and residential homes. Some residential work involves living in – accommodation is provided and you can expect shift work. Day centre work is usually done between the hours of 8.30 am and 6 pm.

Residential Work
Residential care is provided for children, people with physical or

mental handicap and for the elderly – the last group being the biggest. Long-stay residents may know no other home than the institution in which they live and staff have a responsibility to make them feel as much 'at home' as they can and to help them lead as full lives as possible. Some residents need a lot of physical care and you can expect to perform such tasks as dressing, washing, accompanying to the toilet and feeding – you will be surprised how quickly you get used to the more unpleasant tasks – and you should be taught how to lift heavy weights without strain.

Great efforts are made to keep children out of long-term care and, whenever possible, they are sent to small, family-size homes. Those who do end up in care will probably not be easy to look after; they could be suffering from neglect and/or abuse and may display behavioural problems – for example, they might be withdrawn or disruptive – arising from their earlier experiences or from separation from their parents and familiar surroundings. Staff have to try to provide a stabilising influence in their lives and can do this by sharing meals with them, talking and listening to them, supervising their homework and recreation, organising activities and teaching the older ones to become independent.

Handicapped people may be suffering from physical or mental handicap or both. Those suffering from physical handicap only are likely to want to be as independent and autonomous as possible and many people with mental handicap are also able to achieve a fair amount of independence. Some severely mentally handicapped people present distressing symptoms – you need a particular kind of resilience to work with them, but it can be very rewarding.

Different sorts of residential accommodation are provided for the elderly according to their needs. The most autonomous can manage in sheltered accommodation; this is nearly all provided by a local authority and needs only a warden in charge. It usually consists of self-contained living units, which residents furnish with their own things, and common rooms where they can meet to talk or watch television. Each unit is fitted with an intercom device and the warden makes a daily round to check that no one is ill or needs help. Old people's homes, which may be run by a local authority or a private individual, cater for those who are still active or for those who have suffered physical or mental degeneration. It must be said that in a few old people's homes the residents are not well treated. Find out as much as you can about a place before accepting a job and report any cases of cruelty or neglect to the social services department.

Case Studies
Frances is a warden in council sheltered accommodation.

I spent several years in the Merchant Navy, working first as a stewardess and then in the duty-free shops selling perfume, and I decided to take early retirement; jobs were getting scarce and I thought I should make room for younger people. I didn't know what I was going to do and I saw an advertisement in a local paper: 'Warden wanted for sheltered accommodation'. They were looking for someone with nursing experience and I had that. I did two years' mental nursing but didn't complete my training because I got itchy feet and went to sea instead. I sent off for a form; I didn't think I'd hear any more, but I was called for an interview. They had had a lot of applications and I had a very lengthy inteview – how would I deal with this situation and that situation – but I must have given the right answers because they offered me the job and here I am.

A lot of the time in this job all you need is common sense, but in fact I'd had quite a bit of experience with old people at sea. A great many people send their elderly relatives on cruises; I was quite used to dealing with them. Really what you are is a good neighbour, you're here and you're keeping an eye on things. I check that they are all all right and once a day when I do my rounds. Each flat has an intercom cord and I check that all the cords are hanging down as they should be and that nobody's knotted theirs up to get it out of the way. If I think anyone's poorly then I send for the doctor. If anyone does fall sick I would nurse them for 24 hours. That's what I'm obliged to do; I have to look after them for 24 hours then they become the responsibility of the next of kin. But, of course, you use your discretion – I looked after one elderly lady for several days and she's quite well again now. Most of the residents are very independent and some of them are quite active and get out and about.

You do have to take painful decisions sometimes. We had an old man of 90 living here; he smoked 80 cigarettes a day and was always setting off the fire alarm with his smoke, then he had a fall and he became too much of a responsibility so his doctor, his daughter and I decided he'd be better in an old people's home. I was sorry to see him go as he was a lovely gentleman.

I don't think this would be a job for a very young person; it wouldn't do for anyone who wanted to be out and about a lot. You have to be here, you have to be a bit of a stay-at-home. Usually, the council employs the wife of a married couple. I have my flat, it's very nice but I have to pay rent for it. When there are two people and one of them has a salary from another job, it doesn't work out so expensive.

I haven't decided how long I shall stay here, I'm still feeling my way a bit. I have put some chairs and tables in the garden and they like that, they go and sit outside now, and I've put a dartboard in one of the lounges for the men. One or two people said they'd be interested in whist, but it didn't come to anything. When winter comes I'm hoping I'll be able to get something going.

Susan and Brian are school-leavers and both are working in private old people's homes.

Susan

We always say that the only thing that would tell a visitor this is not a hotel is all the sticks and walking frames there are around the place. Many of our residents are very active; one lady does a lot of pruning in the garden and one of our gentlemen walks a mile into the village twice a day. Our youngest resident is 65, but is one of the least mobile because of a stroke, and our oldest is 97. I came here straight from school; my mum does night duty here three nights a week. One week I work from 8 am till 2 pm and the next from 2 pm till 8 pm. We start by serving breakfast, then we clear up and put the plates in the dishwasher and go up and make the beds. That takes quite a long time as we have to change the sheets if someone has wet the bed and there are commodes to empty. Then we see whose bath day it is and we supervise the person's bath; we help them in and out of the bath and we're very careful to see they don't slip. The residents get a cup of tea or coffee at 11 am and we usually grab one too. We do the residents' washing here so we round up the dirty clothes and put them in the machines and at 12 it's time to lay the tables and serve lunch. At 2 o'clock we're quite ready to sit down and have our lunch and the second shift staff come on and have a cup of coffee with us.

When you're on from 2 till 8 it's not so hectic; you serve tea and you serve supper but you have more time to sit and talk to the residents – that's part of your job too. There's a homely atmosphere here; most of the people are very nice. We had one difficult lady, she was always complaining – you couldn't do anything right for her. Then she left and we found out she'd been in four homes before she came to us – she's probably been in four more by now! I like being on duty on Sunday evenings; one of the staff plays the piano and we sing all the old favourites – the residents love it.

Brian

The people who live here suffer from senile dementia. They are not bedridden or anything like that, but they're confused and don't know where they are or sometimes who they are. They don't always recognise members of their family – that upsets them and often they stop visiting. Some of them are quire active and you have to be very careful they don't escape. The doors are always kept locked and all staff carry a big bunch of keys round their waist. Some of my friends think it must be awful working here, but it isn't. Old people with senile dementia are like children, you have to tell them to put on a coat when they go out or ask them if they need to go to the toilet. Sometimes they cry or fly into tantrums, or two of them will have a fight over a chair they both want. One old man spends hours and hours colouring pictures in a colouring book. You need to be very patient – they tell you the same thing over and over again, and old people simply can't be rushed.

People don't stay in this kind of work for very long; it's not very well paid and there are no prospects. I'd like to do nursing but I don't have enough O levels and I'm not very good at exams.

Hostels

Hostels are provided by local authorities, voluntary organisations and the probation service, for the short-term care of those with special needs, eg homeless young people, alcohol and drug abusers, battered women and their children, and ex-prisoners. They are usually run by a team consisting of social workers, care assistants and catering staff, and your duties will depend on the kind of residents the hostel takes in.

Day Care

Day-care centres are for babies and young children, mentally or physically handicapped people, or old people, who are able to live at home but need looking after during the day. House-bound people can easily become bored or depressed and they need a change of scene and new stimuli. Trained staff are usually in charge of day centres, which also employ other trained professionals, eg occupational therapists and care assistants. There are activities – organised play for children, crafts, games, entertainment, drama, music and movement, keep-fit exercises – and care staff help out with these and encourage the centre's users to make the most of everything that is provided. Care staff also do the routine work such as helping wheelchair users in and out of the centre, serving meals, feeding those who cannot feed themselves, accompanying people to the toilet, mopping up spills and making sure everyone is contented.

One criticism levelled at day centres for the elderly is that they provide nothing in the way of intellectual stimulation and that those who organise the activities and/or entertainment seem to assume that old people have stopped being able to think and are interested only in cups of tea and bingo. Many more old people would be drawn into day centres if, occasionally, a thought-provoking activity were laid on.

Home Helps

Home helps are employed by local authorities to assist those who, temporarily or permanently, cannot manage alone. The most common tasks they perform are cooking, cleaning, washing and ironing, shopping, and collecting pensions, but occasionally their duties are similar to those of a nursing auxiliary and include washing, dressing and feeding clients. 'Regulars' may be elderly or handicapped people whom the home help sees once or several times a week; temporary clients are people who just need a hand to get them through a period of convalescence or crisis. In addition to the actual work they do, home helps also act as a vital link between the house-bound client and the outside world; they bring in neighbourhood news and when a doctor or social worker is needed they call one in.

Case Study
Jean has been a local authority home help for 13 years.

I can't stay under one roof all day, or bear going to the same place always and I didn't want to work *all* the time, or else I couldn't look after my own home, but I wanted to meet a lot of folk and do something useful. So I went down to the social services office and applied. You can do as many hours as you like. Now I go to some regulars, and a few emergencies, and there's plenty of variety, but the satisfaction is knowing I'm always helping someone, even if they don't always seem to appreciate it! You clean up their place, you do their main shopping if they can't get out, you do a bit of washing and ironing if they want you to, and you do a lot of listening, as well as a bit of talking. Most of my people are elderly, and usually disabled, so they can't get around easily. Mostly they're alone, and seeing someone to get gossip from and tell things to helps keep them from depression and feeling too lonely. The old people like to see someone young and lively around the place. They often get very fond of you and your family, becoming like grandparents sometimes.

You need to be a good time-keeper because the old people look forward to your coming and get very upset if things aren't as planned. You need to be quite a patient and cheerful person, because sometimes they are feeling poorly and get bad tempered, or they are grieving for a lost husband or wife and feel low, and you have to encourage them. Sometimes you get a chance to help out in a young family where the mother might be in hospital, or having a baby, or recovering from an accident. Then you can look after the children as well, and some of my colleagues sometimes even stay overnight where some temporary care is needed. I always think if I'd started earlier I'd be well prepared now for a proper social work course and really be able to put a lot into that work, knowing what I do about people and their problems, and practical ways to help them.

Drivers

Drivers are, of course, employed in a great many areas of work, but if you are interested in a driving job with a 'social' bias ask what is available with your local authority. Drivers may be needed for vehicles (sometimes adapted to carry handicapped passengers) used to take people to and from day centres, to take children to special schools or to deliver meals to the housebound.

Case Study
Bob is a meals-on-wheels van driver in local authority service.

I wouldn't drive the van if it was coal in the back. No, we are making contact every day with people who really need it, stuck alone in their houses for one reason or other, usually because they are disabled or very old. We don't only bring in their hot dinner from the central kitchens, probably the only cooked food they get, but we hear their tales and have a laugh with them. You've got to be punctual in the work - the food doesn't keep hot for ever, though the vans are specially adapted of course, but also the people come to rely on you coming and get upset if you're erratic. You get to know their habits too, and often we're the ones who become alerted first of all to a real emergency - where someone's fallen over alone and can't get up, been taken ill and needs a doctor or an ambulance, or even, occasionally, has died. One of us (we work in pairs) goes in and stays, in cases like that, while the other gets appropriate help from the emergency services, say, police or ambulance.

In any case, every day when we finish the round we make a report to the supervisor on all the clients. We say if they look a bit poorly perhaps, or if they ask us to pass a message to help them get something - maybe a bit of shopping or help with their bills, or a visit from the doctor. We have to collect the money for the meals and hand it in too, which is a responsibility. You can start out riding alongside the driver, and take a course of driving lessons paid for by the Council while you're on the job, if you prefer that side of it. I think I would be very well prepared now, after five years' experience going in and out of people's homes and seeing to their needs, to train as a professional social worker. Getting to know people, doing the odd turn for them and helping, it makes me feel good. It's like getting paid for what you'd want to do for people anyway. The reward is in the contact with them, the laughs, and when they say 'Thank you dear' and you know they really mean it.

Training

All employees should receive basic on-the-job training from those already doing the work. There are courses that can be taken by school-leavers with no academic qualifications, which will prepare them for caring work and possibly enable them to negotiate a higher salary. See Chapter 8 for details.

Chapter 3

Professional Social Work

The best-known staff in the social services are the social workers themselves; they come from widely differing backgrounds and many of them have had experience in other areas of work. The social services, and other agencies employing qualified social workers, are called upon to deal with a great range of problems concerning, for example, adoption and fostering, children placed in care, children with behavioural problems, young people in trouble with the law, alcohol and drug abusers, the elderly living at home or in institutions, those suffering from chronic or acute mental illness, hospital patients, the physically and mentally handicapped, the homeless, people with housing problems and families in crisis situations. Social workers have to bring a practical approach to such problems and, at the same time, be able to win the confidence of clients – not all of whom will be cooperative – with whom they try to build up a trusting relationship. Clients come from all walks of life so you must feel at ease, and be able to communicate, with people from any social or ethnic group as well as with other professionals.

Social work agencies are empowered by law to intervene in the lives of people when the situation demands it; this may mean that an approved (ie, specially trained) social worker will decide to place a child in care or to play a part in the hospitalisation of someone who is mentally ill.

A lot of the time social workers work on their own, taking decisions and planning how they use their time, but they are very much team members and work closely with their own departmental colleagues and with other professionals such as doctors, teachers, health visitors, occupational therapists and the police. There will be an office base where paperwork and administration are done, but most of a social worker's day is spent seeing clients in hospitals, residential institutions or day centres and, of course, making home visits. It is while making a home visit that you may occasionally encounter unpleasant or difficult situations; clients can be obstructive, abusive or violent and sometimes live in filthy, and even infested, houses or flats. You do not have to face such situations alone; the environmental health service, the police and your professional colleagues will support you.

Some clients' problems cannot be dealt with by any practical course of action but can be alleviated by counselling. People can be helped to change their attitudes or modify certain behaviour patterns or to come to terms with a handicap. A social worker must be the kind of person that someone with a problem can talk to and who will be detached enough to give objective advice.

The social services are organised to meet local needs and it is not fashionable in the profession to use labels such as 'field' or 'medical' social worker. A social worker is a social worker – all hold the CQSW or DipSW (see pp 86 and 93) – and are usually organised to deal with a wide range of client groups. However, there are certain well-defined work settings, so for convenience I will outline the work under the headings field, residential, medical, psychiatric and community social work. (In Scotland the local authority social work departments are, in addition, responsible for providing probation and after-care services.)

Field Social Work

Social workers employed by a local authority social services department are usually members of an area team which may include welfare assistants, an occupational therapist, a home-help organiser and clerical staff, all under the direction of an area team leader. They are based at an office but will not necessarily spend much time there each week. Office duties will include paperwork (letter writing and form filling), dealing with callers and telephone inquiries, attending case conferences and meetings, and liaising with statutory or voluntary agencies.

When a social worker takes on a case, the first thing he/she has to do is to make an assessment, that is, decide on the appropriate course of action. It may be a question, for example, of giving an elderly client advice about claiming benefits or of taking urgent steps to deal with a sudden domestic crisis.

Much of a social worker's time is spent arranging services for clients; for example, a care package including a home help and meals on wheels could enable an elderly client to remain in his/her own home; or single parents with very young children or young people with a drug problem could be greatly helped by attending a self-help or support group.

Your caseload will contain all sorts of clients with a wide range of problems but, if you worked for a local authority in an inner city where social conditions were very poor, you could find yourself mostly helping families in crisis or dealing with children at risk; in a rural area the majority of your clients would probably be elderly.

Case Study
Monica works for a local authority in a rural area.

I am part of a team consisting of six social workers, a senior social worker, a craft instructor, a welfare assistant and a clerical officer, based at a sub-office. Most of the time, of course, I am out and about working on my own. The work is extremely varied and that is, I think, what makes it so demanding and interesting. To give you some idea of what it is like I can tell you about a typical day.

I leave home at 8.15 am and start work, officially, at 8.45. I go into the office and usually the first job is to pick up messages that have been left from the previous day. I spend until around 10.30 sorting out the backlog and preparing for the day's visits. There is one clerical person who serves everyone at the office, so the amount of clerical assistance is very small and I find myself writing out my letters in longhand – I don't actually type them myself. There are quite a lot of letters as a great deal of the work involves other people, asking for help from other agencies, that sort of thing, because our work is largely assessment and co-ordination, and action planning. There is a lot of internal clerical work to do. For example, if an occupational therapist or home help is needed this has to be logged on the appropriate form in triplicate.

Today, in fact, I was stuck in the office till about 11.30 and then I went out to see an old lady. The initial referral in this case had come from a relative, who had contacted me to tell me of the old lady's plight. My assessment, after talking to the relative on the telephone, was that the lady was going to need some financial advice and perhaps some raising of finance. I went round and saw the lady and that's what my work is going to be, that's the plan we worked out together.

One afternoon a week I work at the local GPs' surgery. Here I am doing intake work directly on the 'patch'; people do not have to come to the office or have a home visit arranged in order to have contact with a social worker. It also improves communication with the other members of the primary health care team – nurses, health visitors and GPs. This morning I was meant to be at the surgery at 11.30, but I was late. My next visit was to a chap whose wife had walked out leaving him with two young children. I was seeing him for the first time; he had had to go to the doctor to get signed off work and the doctor had suggested he made an appointment to see me. I had not had the opportunity of getting this referral from the doctor formally, of discussing it with him, so I went into it cold and I shall link up with the doctor afterwards.

When I'd seen that chap I went to the hospital to see about the discharge of one of my clients who had been there for some time. I had to reactivate the care package that enables her to stay at home and that had been put on ice while she was in hospital. Then there was a visit to another elderly lady to give her news of the financial help I'd arranged for her and to offer support on some other matters. Lunch, by the way, was some biscuits eaten in the car; I always keep a packet in the car.

After that there was a meeting at a council old people's home, which finished rather earlier than I thought it would, so by 3 o'clock I was doing some phoning from the home and then I popped off and made another visit to an old chap I'd managed to get rehoused – I'm still sorting out the finances relating to that move and making sure he's comfortable and setting things up in preparation for the winter.

The vast majority of my work is with old people who present a great range of problems, so you do need a lot of information at your fingertips. After qualification our training is ongoing and I attend lots of courses and seminars on special subjects. I also attend a number of meetings, things like the foster parents' group and a relative support group that I have organised; they meet once a month. I also represent the social services at local meetings of voluntary organisations. I go to day clubs, day centres, and support and therapy groups – in particular those for the elderly or for people with mental health problems.

I do it because I enjoy it. I made up my mind when I was young that I wanted to be a social worker, I went all out to get trained and become as much involved as I could. After I'd been working for some time, I left to have my family and then I returned. I can't imagine doing anything else. I did try a short spell of nursing, but it wasn't for me.

Residential Social Work

You can do residential social work in day centres, residential homes and certain kinds of hostel. Day centres provide day care and support services for people who cannot cope on their own and who might otherwise have to live in an institution. These centres may be multi-purpose or may serve the needs of a single group, such as the mentally handicapped or elderly. Residential homes are provided by local authorities, voluntary organisations and private individuals and they cater mainly for children, the handicapped and the elderly. Hostels are used by people with both acute and long-term problems, for example, the homeless, ex-prisoners, alcoholics, drug addicts and battered women.

Social workers are part of a team consisting of care assistants, kitchen and domestic staff, and possibly teachers, therapists, doctors, psychologists, psychiatrists and others. A senior post in a residential home may be a live-in post, in which case self-contained accommodation would be provided. Non-residential staff may be requested to sleep in a certain number of nights per week. Work settings will vary considerably; some premises are purpose-built, others are in converted houses and may be neither comfortable nor convenient.

Wherever you are based, you will be involved in casework, assessing the needs of individual clients, counselling them, and helping them make the best of their lives and achieve as much independence as possible. You will do group work, organising discussion and self-help groups and group activities. The day-to-day care of residents will include sharing meals with them, seeing children off to school, helping the physically handicapped to wash and dress, and arranging medical care. On the administrative side you will run the home, manage and train support staff, liaise with other professionals, write reports, and attend meetings and case conferences.

Residential care is generally seen as a last resort and clients may not be easy to work with. For example, the children in a residential home may be disturbed adolescents for whom a foster home cannot be found or may be younger and suffering from severe behavioural problems; the old people could be suffering from partial or total loss of their mental faculties and, in addition, be incontinent and/or bedridden; mentally handicapped adults and adolescents can be very strong and may need to be physically restrained. There are always people on hand to help, but the work can be physically and emotionally very taxing.

The atmosphere in a residential home will depend entirely upon the people who run it; a grim-looking building might house an informal 'family' community, whereas in a seemingly ideal setting residents may be very strictly regimented.

Case Study
Bernard is organiser of a residential assessment centre for children in care of the local authority.

After plenty of experience in the social services, as a teacher and as a community worker, I found I wanted a job which offered the chance for really close work with adolescents, especially with those in trouble. Most adolescents living in community homes today are people with real problems, frequently associated with their families. The state of simply being without a family is far less frequent now, and is usually dealt with by children being adopted. So you can expect that those fetching up in residential care will have serious disabilities, not just physical, but social, even psychiatric, which makes working and living with them very tough and demanding.

That being so, you need to know you have the opportunity to get away, and the fact is that having your home tied to your place of work can be a big disadvantage. It can affect your recreation and private life adversely, and also it can affect your attitude to the work itself, and the employer.

However, if you can find a satisfactory way round this (and more and more employers are recognising the problem), the rewards of intensive work with a young person, and increasingly with the parents and family too, to try and modify the attitudes and behaviour which cause him or her so much trouble with the rest of society, can be great. If you know that by your efforts you can help a young person, already in a lot of strife with his or her family, perhaps also with teachers and the police, to adapt and become a well-adjusted citizen, it's great. It means intensive work, self-control, great sympathy with and sensitivity to young people's aspirations and to family relationships, and a great understanding of what makes people able to cope or not with the circumstances of their own lives.

We like to work with child *and* family, watching how they behave together, and then the child's behaviour when alone with us, and help the parents to alter their reactions so that eventually they can learn to live together. Then we become unnecessary!

Medical Social Work

Social workers are found in hospitals, hospices, out-patient clinics, health centres and GPs' surgeries. Their job is to identify the social factors connected with or contributing to a patient's condition and to take steps to alleviate or eliminate as many as possible of his/her problems. They interview patients and sometimes liaise with other professionals in order to assess their needs and draw up a plan of action. As well as the basic general skills of social work, medical social workers need some specific knowledge about illness and disability. Many patients require only short-term help; for example, if a mother is in hospital temporary arrangements may have to be made for the care of children. On the other hand, when serious illness such as cancer or AIDS strikes, both patients and their families may need counselling and practical advice. Stroke or heart-attack patients often have to change their way of life radically; a social worker can help them come to terms with permanent disability or restricted mobility and suggest ways in which a house might be modified eg by turning a downstairs room into a bedroom.

Social workers are trained to work with the terminally ill and with bereaved families. There are a number of formalities that have to be dealt with when a person dies and a social worker can provide immediate practical support at a different and painful time and can follow this up with counselling.

Case Study
Karen is a social worker in a large general hospital.

When I graduated at the age of 21, I took what seemed a sensible step and began training as a chartered accountant. The firm I joined, however, was not very stimulating and, as I'd obtained quite a good degree, I decided to leave and do postgraduate work in criminology instead. Before starting I did some social work in a children's home for a short time and when I'd got my Diploma in Criminology I joined the Home Office as a researcher and stayed four years working, among other things, on indictable sexual offences and on bail hostels. I learned a lot but found the work rather arid and eventually left to train as a probation officer and that's how I got into social work. I was a probation officer for four years, having first completed my CQSW on a postgraduate course. I then left to have a family, but, as I couldn't go back and do part-time work, I did some short-term research contracts into different things, one of which was on the placement of children in residential care.

Now I'm doing local authority work in a general hospital. I do not consider myself as 'a medical social worker', I just happen to be working in a hospital and have become familiar with the sort of problems that people in hospital with medical problems present, but I think my experience gives me the confidence to go out into the field and tackle any sort of problem.

I work in the medical unit of this hospital and cover five wards and a number of clinics so I would not know the circumstances of everyone who comes into these wards and we rely on 'social meetings'. After the main weekly ward round, when all the medical and nursing staff visit their patients and discuss treatment, plan what's going to happen and think about discharge, there is a social meeting at which the social circumstances of a patient are discussed. Not every patient is discussed in detail, but we go through the names in the ward and when the medical staff think there's an elderly patient who might not be able to cope at home, or a young mother whose illness might make it difficult for her to care for her family, or someone seems worried as a result of their illness or diagnosis, they tell us. It is a bit haphazard and depends a lot on the medical or nursing staff interpreting the patients' circumstances. Sometimes clients are referred to us by someone who is working with them and uncovers a problem with which they think we might be able to help. These can often be practical problems, but sometimes they are emotional or domestic problems. We also receive referrals from the out-patient clinics. I then go and see the patient and perhaps say, 'the medical staff would like me to see you because of this or that'. For example, I've just seen an elderly lady who's going out next week; I had a chat and checked that everything was going to be okay and I met her family and they confirmed that there were no problems that we needed to be involved in. Quite often there are purely practical problems to deal with; someone might need a home help or meals on wheels. If it's just a matter of restarting these the ward staff can cope, but if it's the first time we have to get details and then contact the community services. We do sometimes get refusals from the home-help service, which is very hard-pressed, and the client has to struggle on and that's very unsatisfactory from our point of view.

I do some visiting, not so much to see people's living conditions as to offer some support – what you might call after-care – and I've always found that it can be very helpful. It's not just for older people, it might be for very ill younger people and I might mobilise support in the community or link up with a voluntary organisation that could help.

We tend to organise ourselves around the ward social meetings and around the clinics we are involved in. Sometimes I'm rushed off my feet and at other times there's a lull if the wards are fairly quiet. You just have to arrange your time in a way that enables you to pick up emergencies as well as handling your normal caseload.

I think counselling is a very important part of our work and for me it is the most satisfying side of the work, much more so than the purely practical side, such as fixing up with local resources and fiddling around with the DHSS. You are not always involved in a medical problem; it might just come out that a patient had an awful lot of other problems – domestic or marital problems – that might be affected or exacerbated by ill health. Sometimes a consultant or some other member of the medical staff will discover that a person has a problem with their partner or with their children and will refer that patient to us for counselling or advice, or to link up with another agency that can help.

I suppose I can say that I deal with a wide cross-section of people, but there are rather more elderly patients, as a large percentage of admissions to this hospital are elderly patients. There is great pressure in the departments I work in to clear the beds; for every bed that goes empty there is someone waiting in casualty, so we do get very much involved in practical problems, whereas in the geriatric or rehabilitation units they work in a different way and there is more chance to build up relationships with patients. My own work has expanded since I've been here – I still have the responsibilities I started with, but I've taken on others. Some of my colleagues, who have been here a long time, have moved around and worked in different parts of the hospital and I think that's a very good thing. I don't know how long I shall stay here; in a way I find it limiting, but on the other hand, it is very satisfying to be part of a very caring medical team. I see too many things wrong with the system – not so much with this hospital – but with the bureaucracy and the organisation of the social services. I think I'd find it too frustrating to go up the hierarchy and try to do something about it, so maybe I'll branch out and do something more academic. You could say that I'm not typical.

Psychiatric Social Work

There are two main work settings for those interested in psychiatric social work: child guidance clinics or child psychiatry units, and psychiatric units or psychiatric hospitals. In the former, a team consisting of social workers, child psychiatrists and child psychologists works with disturbed children and adolescents. Most of the referrals come from GPs and will probably include those with behavioural problems or with some sort of phobia, disruptive teenagers, withdrawn children, and children with learning problems causing them perhaps to get behind with school work or to play truant. The social workers would make an assessment of the social factors contributing to the problem and would most probably get involved with the whole family to offer family therapy and other kinds of intervention. In some cases they would liaise with teachers, educational welfare officers and educational psychologists.

In a psychiatric unit or psychiatric hospital, social workers meet various different client groups, but the majority of the patients would be elderly people suffering from senile dementia or depression. They help the psychiatrist assess a new referral, work out what the problem is and what has led up to it. It might be that an in-patient would be better off back at home, in which case the social worker would set up a support package consisting of, eg, home helps, meals on wheels and day care, or could be more easily looked after in some sort of residential home, in which case the social worker would try to find a suitable place.

Families of such patients often need both counselling and help with practical arrangements.

Nowadays, the average in-patient's stay in an acute admission ward is not very long, because, whenever possible, he/she is helped to return to living in the community. The social worker assesses the social factors, which may have had quite a lot to do with causing the illness, and would be involved in making the decision about where the patient should be placed in the long term. Some chronic patients are referred to a long-stay psychiatric ward, others can live independently with a lot of community support, returning only when things break down. All sorts of factors can trigger acute mental breakdown - financial, housing, marital or family problems - and a social worker has the task of trying to find solutions or to alleviate them. Certain psychotic conditions create social problems; for example, a manic-depressive in a manic phase may go out and spend all the family income in one hour or get into trouble with the police, or, when severely depressed, might have stopped looking after him/herself and built up enormous rent arrears. These and other problems could well fall to the lot of the social worker to sort out.

Small numbers of social workers also work in other specialist settings. For example, there are social work departments in special hospitals such as Broadmoor and in regional secure units for the mentally ill. They have an important role to play in psychiatric day centres and may also be found in drug dependency clinics, drug advice centres and drinking problem clinics. Social workers can contribute to patients' therapeutic programmes if, for instance, they are interested in group work or one-to-one counselling. And those interested in educational work can get involved in, say, teaching the medical and nursing staff about the part social factors can play in psychiatric illness.

A minority of psychiatric in-patients are admitted compulsorily. This is done by means of medical recommendation, usually by the patient's GP and a psychiatrist, together with an application for admission, to be made either by an approved social worker (one specially trained for this area of work), or by the nearest relative. It is usually felt to be good practice to take the responsibility away from the family and involve an approved social worker.

Case Study

Jonathan is a psychiatric social worker in the field of 'deliberate self-harm'.
His job is not typical of psychiatric social work, but any social worker can expect to work occasionally with the kind of clients with whom he works exclusively.

Psychiatric social work was always my main interest; a large part of the CQSW course is practical placements and most courses say that one main placement should be in a social services area office and I did that; for my other I chose to work in a psychiatric hospital.

For two years now I've been working full time in the field of 'deliberate self-harm'. I get my referrals from the local district hospital and I work with people who have perhaps taken an overdose or made other suicidal gestures. About a third of these people are treated in the accident service as they are not seriously ill and don't need to be admitted to hospital; when they are discharged from the accident service, if the medical staff feel they have problems I can deal with, they get in touch with me and I contact them at home. Most of the others are admitted to medical wards, either because they are quite bad physically or because they've got a lot of problems going on and it seems a bit risky to send them home again. Those who are the most severely depressed or suicidal are referred straight away to the psychiatrists, but the majority are referred to me and my first job is to make an assessment of their psychological state, to work out what the level of suicidal intent was and then to advise the medical staff on whether the patient is going to be ready for early discharge and, if they are ready, to work out a plan for further help. Quite often, not much intervention is needed – I might just give them my name and phone number and tell them they're welcome to get in touch if they run into problems in the future – at other times there are specific problems that I try to help them with, obviously with their agreement, and we work out a plan of action.

Some individuals are particularly vulnerable – they may have had a deprived background or adverse life events going back a long way – and they've become prone to depression and are particularly impulsive. A number of people who deliberately harm themselves are suffering from clear-cut psychiatric disorders, most commonly a depressive illness. Depression is a very complex business. I am particularly interested in psychological treatments rather than medical ones. People who are depressed may have obvious social problems, for example, they could have got badly into debt or have housing problems. I am involved in a lot of negotiations to get people rehoused. Unlike some parts of the country, this area is very well off for resources and I quite often refer a client to another service if I know there is a good one, I spend a great deal of time liaising with other agencies. Depression is often related to marital problems and, although there is a marriage guidance service, I see it as part of my job as a social worker to offer marriage guidance counselling myself. If I am very worried about someone being suicidal I get in touch with my psychiatrist colleagues and ask them to see the client, or I may try to involve the psychiatric day clinic or the drink problems clinic or the drug dependency unit or different sorts of social club. A social worker has to have very up-to-date knowledge of all the resources available and make sure that clients are aware of what's on offer.

I carry a bleep; the medical staff can always get hold of me, so you can say I'm permanently on duty. I have a small office and I start my day there as I try to get people to know that if they want to contact me by phone I'm in between 9 and 11. A tremendous amount of phoning both in and out goes on in that time and I also try to do my paperwork and catch up with admin. I've usually got two or three people to see at the hospital, maybe a new referral for me to assess, or someone I'm already involved with, so I may go over there in the second half of the morning and I'll probably have lunch there. In the afternoon there may be one or two clients who come to my office for counselling of one sort or another, and in the second half of the afternoon I may well have home visits to make. If there are children involved I see them after school; most of my home visits are made at four, five, or even six o'clock.

Working in the field of mental health has always been my particular interest so in, say, ten years' time I wouldn't mind being perhaps a senior social worker on a psychiatric unit. But I think it wouldn't be a very good thing to do social work as a career for 30 or 40 years. Social work is basically about one human being responding to another, and if you are responding to people's problems and distress day in day out for a number of years it would be very difficult to retain that natural human response, so I've got a lot of doubts about carrying on in the social services for a very long time. What many people do is become managers; they go up the hierarchy. What I myself might be doing in 20 years' time I cannot say.

Community Social Work

Some social workers specialise in working with groups of clients who have a common problem, such as bad housing, unemployment, lack of local facilities, or who are a minority group within the community, eg, an ethnic minority. They initiate or support remedial action and use their knowledge, professional contacts and the resources they can summon to help a group, which might otherwise be relatively powerless, tackle its problems. They also act as a link between the clients and the relevant voluntary organisations and/or local authority department. Some community workers see their role as a branch of social work; others stress their detachment from it. Titles include neighbourhood worker, social development officer, community development officer and community social worker.

Social workers often try to influence social policy and the deployment of resources to favour the disadvantaged and generally to bring about social reform. Whether or not they will be successful in doing this will often depend upon their place of employment.

Opportunities

The biggest employers of social workers are the local authority social services departments in England and Wales, the local authority social work departments in Scotland and the health and social services boards in Northern Ireland; of course, the greatest concentration of jobs is in large towns and cities. Other employers include the large national charities and voluntary organisations (see Chapter 7), local education authorities, universities and colleges, the armed forces and community organisations. *The Social Services Yearbook* gives the addresses of all UK social services departments, voluntary organisations and armed forces social work agencies; advertisements for posts appear in *Social Work Today, New Statesman & Society, Community Care, Public Service and Local Government, The Guardian* (Wednesdays) and the local press.

Conditions of Employment and Prospects

Conditions of employment and the nature of the work vary from one post to another. Many local authorities recognise that the work is stressful and provide a counselling and support service for employees. You can usually progress from a basic-grade post to a managerial, administrative or advisory post. However, some agencies, acknowledging that many people go into social work because they want to work with clients, are creating special posts which allow experienced social workers to continue concentrating on this kind of work. In any case, you will, of course, receive regular salary increments and you can increase your earning power by developing specialisms. You should have the opportunity to attend special subject courses and seminars throughout your career and, with further training and qualifications, you can branch out into specialist work, such as adoption, fostering, and work with the visually handicapped. You can switch from one kind of social work to another or move into other areas such as consultancy or teaching. Opportunities exist for teaching on social work courses in universities and colleges, and for acting as practice tutors to students.

Chapter 4
Allied Professions

The jobs described in this chapter are very much 'social' work, in that they involve working with people – often in their own homes – helping them to improve their circumstances, overcome or come to terms with handicaps, and resolve their problems. Those who practise in these fields have their own professional title, expertise, skills and training.

Education Welfare Work

The Education Welfare Service (EWS) exists to ensure the regular attendance of pupils at school and to help pupils make the most of the educational opportunities available to them. It is concerned with both state and private education. The main duties and responsibilities of an education welfare officer (EWO) are as follows:

☐ To help assess the social, emotional and educational problems that may be hindering a child from benefiting from the available educational opportunities.
☐ To develop and support relationships and understanding between children, parents and teachers.
☐ To try to solve or alleviate problems of poor attendance, material deprivation, or disruptive behaviour.
☐ To offer help and advice to parents of children with handicaps and special needs.
☐ To work closely with other agencies concerned with child welfare, especially with regard to cases of child abuse, schoolgirl pregnancies, drug dependency and glue sniffing.
☐ To call and participate in case conferences and meetings.
☐ To give information on the facilities available for children needing special educational placement.

☐ To see that appropriate action is taken in cases of non-attendance at school.

☐ To see that all relevant information is submitted for intended proceedings in Magistrates' or Juvenile Courts.

☐ To see that the by-laws relating to the part-time employment of school children are applied.

☐ To issue licences for children participating in entertainment and to check the conditions in which they will be working.

☐ To advise on education other than at school.

☐ To advise on and negotiate transfers of children between schools.

☐ To advise on and participate in suspensions and expulsions.

☐ To undertake escort duties.

☐ To inform families about their entitlement to free meal awards and other welfare benefits.

Obviously, the amount of time devoted to each of these activities will vary considerably from one EWO to another, but it can be said that home or school visiting may take up to 70 per cent of their time, whereas escort duties or matters relating to child employment will probably occupy only 3 per cent or less.

Officers see themselves as a school's or a parent's first point of contact for help. They work closely with teachers, the child guidance service, probation officers, the police, voluntary agencies, youth services and with social workers employed by social services departments. A few authorities have integrated their EWS into the social services, but the great majority have retained the EWS within education. In some areas EWOs are school-based and in others they are office-based and make regular visits to the schools on their patch. Referrals may come from a school, eg in cases of suspected child abuse, or from parents, eg in cases of unhappiness at school. Like all social workers, EWOs have a very varied working day, dividing their time between paperwork and administration, meetings and case conferences, and school and home visits. In addition to professional competence, the work calls for comon sense, sensitivity and the ability to communicate with those of a different ethnic or cultural background.

At present there is no professional training specific to education welfare work. The most commonly accepted qualification is the CQSW or DipSW (see pp 86 and 93) but other appropriate qualifications, eg teaching, and/or relevant work experience are also accepted. The professional body is the National Association for Social Workers in Education. In-service training courses for

EWOs are run in various parts of the country. Career structure, conditions of employment and salaries vary from authority to authority. There are opportunities for promotion to the post of senior EWO or principal EWO.

Case Study
Tom is an Education Welfare Officer who has had three years' experience with two city education authorities.

After having several short-term jobs in this country and abroad, which I took when I graduated in politics from university, I joined the city Education Welfare Service with no clear idea of what the job entailed, nor any particular desire to work with young people and their families.

I had a good induction training at the outset and now I find the work demanding and absorbing with opportunities to work with families in their own homes, which is the part I most enjoy. I find my previous varied work experience, plus my non-specialist degree, help me avoid getting bogged down in jargon and being too narrow in my approach to youngsters in trouble at school.

I start, of course, by focusing on a child's school attendance problems, to see how we can best help him or her get the most out of school. Frequently, when attendance is very poor, the pressure is on to take the parents to court for an order requiring them to present the child for schooling - but I see the work as doing everything possible to avoid that extreme. One 11-year-old boy, for instance, wasn't attending school at all, but it turned out, when we visited, that his elderly father was very ill and in fact died shortly afterwards. After the death, the boy found it quite possible to attend school regularly again, and court action would have been most inappropriate, adding tremendous strain to an already burdened family.

The work isn't suitable for the very young person, as it deals with all sorts of family matters which take a bit of maturity to cope with, nor is it for the weak-spirited. Things can take an unpredictable turn, with rare cases of quite violent reaction to your visiting the home and concerning yourself with a young person's problems. You need to be able to assume authority with youngsters and to support and counsel their parents, often over a long period. You need to know all the other agencies in the district too, as frequently you have neither the specialist skills nor the time to spend with a family requiring help. It's important to be familiar with child guidance, educational psychology, social and health services, to have the maximum effect on a young person's approach to, and opportunities for, learning. So you spend a lot of time with other professionals, primarily, of course, teachers, working out a programme for a child and his or her family between you all. It may seem time-consuming and even wasteful, but it's vital for the child.

Youth and Community Work

Youth and community work is geared towards social education and is financed mainly by education authorities. Most authorities employ a youth and community officer who is responsible for co-ordinating the work in the area, and there will be a team of youth workers to carry out the tasks. As well as this statutory provision there is a strong voluntary movement, often partly financed by the education authorities but operating independently. Youth work is undertaken mainly with the 14 to 18 age group and can be done in a variety of settings.

There are two main minds of job: centre-based and detached. A centre-based worker is one who runs a youth centre or club in much the same way as a warden runs a community centre. He or she is responsible for administration and co-ordination of the activities of the centre. A detached worker does not have a physical base but goes out into the community to talk to the young people in the streets, the cafes, the discos and wherever else they congregate. He or she must make contact with young people who for one reason or another do not want to come to a club, and must know the area well because this is the working arena.

Both these kinds of workers have the same basic aim – to help the adolescents they deal with to develop social skills and good personal relationships and to grow up with a greater awareness of themselves and their society.

As a youth worker you must, first of all, be able to establish yourself as an adult friend with whom all kinds of things can be discussed freely. You must, of course, have a good knowledge of the way society and our political system work, and you must also know the local community well. You do not 'teach' in any formal sense but you should be able to impart information and stimulate discussion in an informal way so that the youngsters you work with can make judgements for themselves. Leisure is also an important aspect of the work, as it is the failure to use leisure time constructively that often leads young people into trouble. Your role may be to provide the right kinds of activities at your own centre, or to direct youngsters to suitable activities available elsewhere in the community. Either way, you need to know your youngsters well and have good local contacts in places where their needs might be met.

Details of training are set out on pages 99-101.

Health Visiting

Health visitors have a nursing background (see pp 101-3 for details of training) and they are usually members of a primary health team which includes GPs, district nurses, midwives and school nurses. Their job is to assess health care needs in the home and the community, to promote health in the community and to prevent mental, physical and social ill health. They do a lot of work with mothers and babies as they have statutory responsibility for children from birth to the age of five. Before a baby is born, a health visitor will call on the mother and inform her of the services available to her and after the birth will continue to follow the baby's progress. Young mothers may need counselling on anything from weaning to welfare benefits and health visitors can help and advise them, sometimes on a one-to-one basis when they are making a house call or seeing the mother at a clinic, or in a group such as a postnatal support group which they have organised. When child abuse is suspected, a health visitor calls in the support of the social services; the case is investigated, the family counselled and given practical help and, if necessary, the child/children are taken to a place of safety.

Health visitors also make routine visits to the elderly and the handicapped, giving advice on good health practices and, when necessary, will call in the help of statutory or voluntary bodies.

They have an educational role to play too; this may involve such things as visiting schools to give talks on personal hygiene, training medical or nursing students, organising support groups, eg for foster parents, and running parentcraft classes.

Opportunities for Qualified Health Visitors

You can take a short further education refresher course or a specialist course in a subject you find particularly interesting. Employing authorities also offer opportunities for gaining additional experience and keeping in touch with new developments. If you have had a minimum of two years' full-time practice you can take a field-work teacher course and then train student health visitors, or with further training you can become a lecturer in health visiting within the education service. For those who wish to pursue a management career within the NHS, appropriate courses are available.

There are occasional opportunities for health visitors to work overseas with organisations such as Save the Children Fund or the Soldiers', Sailors' and Airmen's Families Association.

Case Study

Morag is a health visitor. Before she started this work she trained as a nurse (an SRN), worked in a hospital and did some private home nursing.

I went into health visiting originally because I wanted to stay in this town and now I like the work for itself. I like seeing the people and getting to know them. I'm attached to a group practice and I'm part of a community team consisting of doctors, physiotherapists, occupational therapists, social workers and community nurses.

My responsibilities are first and foremost to the under-fives. We have to see that they are properly fed and looked after and that there are no developmental delays – things like not speaking or not walking at the right age – and we weigh them regularly and do sight and hearing tests. When a baby is born to a mother who is a patient of the practice, we get a form and we go and see the mother and offer our services and let her know of the services available; the mothers have the right to refuse, but the majority don't. I have never had a refusal; I've always had full cooperation.

We start seeing babies at 28 days – in some places they start at 10 days – we must see them at 28 days, then at six weeks, three months, seven months and yearly after that. I run a well-baby clinic where mothers come to have their babies weighed and can talk to me if they have any problems – if they are worried about things like poor sleeping, crying, tantrums, bed-wetting or diet. I don't deal with coughs and colds, although we do give advice on things like rashes and spots. For all medical things they see the doctor.

When a baby is due for a check we ring the mother or the mother rings us and brings the baby in or I call at the house. It is usually more satisfactory to carry out assessments at home as the child is more relaxed and, in any case, we try to go to the house at least once or twice as we like to see the conditions people are living in and observe family dynamics. The majority of people are pleased to see you and enjoy the visit; you're somebody in authority and at the same time you're close to them and you care what they're doing, so most of the time they're happy to see you. If people are suspicious you try to build a relationship by helping them with difficulties. People often come to me when they've got housing problems or when they want help applying for benefits. Sometimes all they need is someone to talk things through with; we do a lot of just supporting mothers, giving them a bit of confidence in themselves.

I'm lucky in the place I work in; my job is easy because my mothers are mostly very well supported by their families or their extended families. It is different in a city; health visitors there use a different part of their training. All the time they're worried about non-accidental injuries. When they see a child that is bruised, the chances are that the bruises were inflicted by an adult. Identifying the family at risk and preventing maltreatment and child abuse are a very big part of a health visitor's work in places where there are a lot of unsupported mothers or people cohabiting with the wrong sort of people.

I visit the elderly as well, and people living alone or in poor conditions. When I see somebody in need of, say, meals on wheels or a home help, I refer them to an agency or arrange something myself. I keep a watching brief on people and a general surveillance of the elderly in the practice. In this work you draw on all aspects of your training and I'm always on the look out for signs of deterioration, for example swollen ankles, memory failure, unsteadiness in walking, signs that people are getting less able to care for themselves.

The definition of a health visitor's work is 'the prevention of ill health and the promotion of good health'; that's the slogan we work to and really it's a combination of medical and social work.

Occupational Therapy

Occupational therapists (OTs) have a broadly based, medically orientated training (see pp 103-5), which includes practical work in a hospital, and they help their clients to achieve maximum physical, psychological, social and economic independence. They work with those who are temporarily disabled (whether physically or mentally), those with permanent but stable disability, patients suffering from progressive debilitating disorders, people with long-term psychiatric disorders, with children and with the elderly. They are members of a multidisciplinary team involved in various aspects of medical care or rehabilitation, and they can work in a number of environments.

The two main employers are the health service and local authorities, but job opportunities for OTs are expanding into areas such as the prison service and in companies that deal with disabled people or who manufacture equipment for them. An increasing number of occupational therapists are self-employed, and they may be found in clients' homes, in the community, in schools, in the workplace and in a leisure setting.

Some OTs specialise in working with particular groups of clients, eg young children, people who have suffered spinal injury or burns, or work in units treating drug or alcohol abusers. Work with mentally ill clients involves helping them overcome such problems as lack of confidence, anxiety, depression, irrational thoughts and fears, and difficulties in relationships with other people. The OT helps and encourages them to take part in activities which reflect aspects of everyday life. Therapy may include discussion groups, work projects and recreational pursuits, as well as practical activities like shopping and cooking.

OTs employed by a local authority social services department spend about two-thirds of their time visiting clients in their own homes, in residential institutions and in day centres. When they make a home visit they see what adaptations can be made to a house or flat, provide personal aids to daily living and make sure the clients and their families use these correctly. They may continue a treatment programme initiated in hospital to aid rehabilitation. If a client is likely to be able to work, an OT may be called upon to advise a Disablement Resettlement Officer on his/ her interests, aptitudes, working ability and physical or mental limitations. Day centres and residential institutions cater for a number of different client groups and OTs advise on suitable, varied and purposeful programmes of activities that will help clients maximise their mental and physical capacities. OTs who have taken additional training in play therapy may seek employment in child psychiatric centres where they assist medical staff in diagnosis and treatment. Administrative duties and paperwork are usually carried out in the office; these include writing reports, seeing that adaptation work is carried out and liaising with other professionals, agencies or voluntary organisations.

A very important part of any OT's work is counselling and helping clients and their families come to terms with disability. During a course of treatment, which could last weeks or months, they are able to get to know their clients and build up a relationship with them. OTs work on their own and alongside other professionals; they need to be perceptive of their clients' needs and, at the same time, highly practical.

Employment prospects are good; there are more posts than there are trained OTs and, as British qualifications are recognised by the World Federation of Occupational Therapists, it is possible to find work abroad in affiliated countries. After qualifying you can choose either a rotational post which enables you to change from working with children to working with elderly people, say, within a few months, or you can go directly into a specialist area, for example, spinal injury rehabilitation. In the NHS there are a number of management grades leading up to the post of District Occupational Therapist and there are three grades of District Occupational Therapist. With additional qualifications, OTs can move into teaching or research.

Unqualified people can work as OT helpers or assistants under the supervision of a qualified OT in a hospital or in the community. You will be given on-the-job training or, while in post, you can take a course run by the College of Occupational Therapists.

Case Study
Francesca is an OT in a local authority social services department.

After doing A levels, I worked as an assistant OT for a year really to see if that was the career I wanted to do, if I liked working with disabled people, if I liked working in a hospital, which is where most OTs work, and during that time I had the interviews with my training college. If I'd had no experience of working with disabled people I would not have had a chance of getting a place in college.

The training is very broad-based and looks at the wider aspects of disability rather than just its physical effects on a person; it looks at the psychological and social effects of disease. We study in depth such subjects as anatomy, physiology, psychology and psychiatry but, at the same time, we learn practical skills such as woodwork, printing, art and drama, and we use those practical skills in our treatment in a hospital setting or in the community. We do group work and we treat patients individually and might, for example, do this in a workshop. We probably use the same sort of exercises as a physiotherapist would use to treat, say, a wrist injury, but an OT's patients are actually making something and at the end they've got something concrete and that has taken their mind off the fact that it probably hurt while they were doing it, and the exercise wasn't boring - that's one of the differences between the two treatments.

Most OTs work in a hospital but I work in social services in the community. In my training I worked in both general hospitals and psychiatric hospitals, and I could switch my work environment and go back to a hospital without further training. I suppose I spend about half my time at the office and half out in people's homes. I may not be typical because, being a senior, I spend more time in meetings than my colleagues; for them, I imagine, it is about 30 per cent in the office and 70 per cent out with clients. In the office we are writing our reports, chasing up work we have requested and liaising over the telephone; the rest of the time we're out visiting clients in their own homes, in day centres or in residential homes.

We have clients of all ages; the younger children would have conditions such as spina bifida or cerebral palsy, usually resulting from complications at birth, and we also see older children with these disabilities. In the middle age range it tends to be diseases such as multiple sclerosis, motor neurone disease, muscular dystrophy, Parkinson's disease and Huntington's chorea, and with older people the general effects of ageing - arthritis, heart problems and strokes.

I'm particularly interested in clients in the age group 30 to 65 with neuro-progressive disease; for one thing they are more of a challenge. With older people you can go in and provide a rail or a raised toilet seat and that's the end of the problem. With this younger age group you would have a more detailed and a longer involvement with a client and there's the chance to build up a relationship. Also I think I feel more empathetic with that age group.

We often find that when we give someone practical advice or help - for example, we might provide a piece of equipment to help an arthritic lady do a task in the kitchen that previously the home help or a relative was doing - the effect is psychological as well as physical. We may not be making her arthritis better but she's not having to depend on others, she's actually able to bake something for someone else and that's very good for morale.

Counselling skills are often needed on a visit. We won't be asked to visit someone purely to counsel, but because we are involved at a very personal level - we might have to ask a person how they get on and off the loo - during our visit, while we are giving practical advice, we end up having a counselling role too. Because we're sitting with someone in their own home and we're having tea with them, and because we don't appear as 'professional' as the people they have met in hospital - we don't wear uniform - clients find it comfortable to talk about other problems. You're helping people to overcome physical disability and, at the same time, you're helping emotionally with the effects of their disease and helping them to come to terms with their condition. OTs in a hospital have, perhaps, a more practical role; they help people get over a particular disability or prepare them for discharge, and the counselling they do might be at a different level. They will see the patient's relatives and will advise them, but they are in a hospital and the patient's behaviour and feelings of ease are very, very different from what they are at home. When you do a home visit, you might find out different things about a person, things that bothered them but that they couldn't express in the hospital because of the environment.

In order to improve our clients' circumstances we have to liaise with housing departments, with teachers, with non-medical professionals - a very wide range of folk. I enjoy the variety - no two days are alike and no day is ever boring, I enjoy liaising with all the different people and improving the facilities for people with disabilities, and I enjoy the positive feedback you get when you solve a problem. For a small percentage of clients we solve a particular problem, the case is closed and we never hear from them again, though they will tell somebody else of our involvement so obviously the word is spread, but most of our clients come back again and again; those who have got a rapidly deteriorating condition we will be involved with over several months and we will visit regularly.

There are two things that are hard to take. One is working for a bureaucratic department like the social services and the difficulty of getting things done, trying to get through all the various tiers and perhaps in the end having the frustration of not achieving anything. The other is the distress that arises from the people we see; many of them are deteriorating, some very rapidly, and I find it particularly distressing dealing with those who are in the middle age range, or young people who are dying fairly quickly – that's probably the hardest. In fact, you have to toughen yourself a bit because it doesn't help people if you go in and cry with them, but sometimes I go and cry in my car. In the social services department there is a tradition of supervision by managers; they see you once a fortnight or every three weeks and this does not happen in hospital. It's difficult for OTs; the person who supervises me is not an OT and does not have any medical training, so the support and advice I get are quite general and often it would be nice to speak to someone who really understands the difficulties. That kind of support we tend to get from each other and there are also opportunities for certain training courses.

Other

Speech Therapy
This profession is closely linked to medicine, education and psychology; speech therapists treat speech, language and voice defects in patients who may be suffering from congenital deformities, disorders resulting from disease, and psychological or neurological disorders. (Speech therapy should not be confused with elocution which improves poor but normal speech.) Patients are referred by GPs, hospital consultants and teachers; speech therapists diagnose their condition, assess them and devise a course of treatment. Therapy may take place on a one-to-one basis or in groups and a speech therapist has to spend quite a lot of time observing, getting to know and winning the confidence of patients. This is a graduate profession and details can be obtained from the College of Speech and Language Therapists.

Music, Drama and Art Therapies
Music, drama and art can all be used in hospitals and day centres both to provide a source of active enjoyment for patients/clients and as forms of therapy to help those with mental illness or handicap communicate and express themselves. You can take professional training (details of which can be obtained from the British Association of Art Therapists, the Association of Drama Therapists and the British Society for Music Therapy) and there are also openings for unqualified people.

Chapter 5
Working with Offenders

Working with offenders calls for patience and resilience; it can be deeply rewarding, but it can also be very demanding and frustrating. Many people who come into conflict with the law have had a lot to contend with in life; they may have been neglected or abused in childhood, they may have grown up in an environment where crime and/or violence were endemic, they may have come from a broken home or a home in which there was drug abuse or heavy drinking; they may simply lack the most basic skills such as reading, writing, parentcraft and housekeeping. You can do a lot for such people. You can try to act as a stabilising influence in their lives and can help them to acquire some of the skills that most people take for granted which, in turn, will enhance their self-esteem and make them feel less outcast from society. However, do not imagine that offenders will necessarily welcome your efforts to help them. You are just as likely to meet with suspicion or hostility from your clients, and you could have to spend a long time trying to build up a relationship and win their confidence and co-operation.

If you are drawn to the idea of working with offenders because you are full of idealism, you could be very discouraged by some of the things you see and people you come up against; there are still plenty of people in authority who believe that all offenders should be treated harshly, punitively and repressively.

The Probation Service

Probation officers work largely with older delinquent children, young people and adults who have been in conflict with the law. They have been called 'social workers to the courts' but their work is really more broadly based than that. In every area in which they work, they aim to 'advise, assist and befriend' their clients and encourage them towards a more socially acceptable way of life.

Organisation

In England and Wales the Home Office is responsible for the organisation of the probation and after-care service. Probation officers are employed by local probation and after-care committees in 56 areas. In Scotland the local authority social work departments are responsible for providing probation and after-care services. In Northern Ireland the service is administered by a probation board whose membership is broadly based and representative of the community.

To become a probation officer you must hold the CQSW or DipSW (see pp 86 and 93) and you would then join a team which might consist of a senior probation officer (or senior social worker in Scotland) and several main-grade probation officers supplemented with one or more ancillary workers and possibly a social work student on a field placement.

The Work

Probation officers spend part of their time in the office doing paperwork, seeing callers and attending team meetings. Usually there will be one late evening per week when probationers are expected to call and see their probation officer. They can expect to be on duty in court once or twice a week – in some areas there are full-time court specialists – and the rest of the time is taken up with home visits, project supervision and development, visits to people in custody, record keeping and the preparation of social inquiry reports.

Work with the Courts

Court work is one of the basic responsibilities of the probation service. Probation officers help judges and magistrates (and sheriffs in Scotland) determine the appropriate sentence for a defendant. They provide the court with a social inquiry report which gives as complete a picture as possible of a defendant's background, character and attitudes, and state their opinion on the type of sentence to which a defendant might respond. In order to complete one of these reports probation officers have to interview defendants at length and make extensive inquiries into their personal and domestic circumstances. The defendants themselves are not always willing to cooperate and the families of an offender can often be hostile, despite the fact that the probation officer is trying to act in his/her best interest. The defendant has the right to disagree with and challenge the social inquiry report in court.

Supervision in the Community

Another basic responsibility of the probation service is the supervision of offenders in the community. Offenders over the age of 17 are supervised on the authority of one of a number of different statutory orders; these include probation orders, community service orders and suspended sentence orders. If the offender does not cooperate voluntarily with the probation officer assigned to him/her the court can add conditions 'to secure the good conduct of the offender'.

Probation Orders

When the court makes a probation order, an offender is placed under supervision for a period of between six months and three years. This may be simply a question of straightforward supervision and the probationer can continue living at home while remaining in regular contact with his/her probation officer, but sometimes the court imposes extra conditions – for example, there may be a recommendation for psychiatric treatment or for treatment to overcome a drug or drink problem, accommodation in an approved hostel may be needed or the court could require the probationer to attend a day centre at which he or she will learn basic social skills and/or participate in therapy or remedial teaching. The probation service's day centres have to be places where the rules are strictly applied and observed but at the same time the atmosphere needs to be such that it will motivate and encourage probationers to become self-confident and self-reliant.

All supervision entails working closely with individual probationers and, where possible, observing them in their family settings. There are no ready-made solutions to anyone's problems; each case has to be assessed individually. The probation officer tries to gain the probationer's confidence, help him or her recognise the problems and find realistic achievable goals.

Community Service

In certain circumstances offenders over the age of 16 can, if they consent, be ordered to undertake between 40 and 240 hours of unpaid work for the community. Probation officers and ancillary staff have to find a supply of community work and inform the court whether suitable jobs are available for the individual offenders who have been referred to them for assessment. They have to see that the work is carried out satisfactorily and in the required number of hours. Community service is an alternative to a custodial sentence and it is therefore intended to be punitive but it can be a very positive experience for an offender, helping to build up his or her self-esteem and confidence. When it does not work out, he or she has to be dealt with in some other way.

Work with Young People
Young people receive a police caution for certain offences and in such instances a probation officer may be called in to help a young offender keep out of further trouble. Those who offend repeatedly, or who have serious charges brought against them, usually end up in court. The probation officer can be asked to provide a social inquiry report for a juvenile court and to supervise a young person who has been made the subject of a supervision order. This responsibility is shared with local authority social services departments. If the court required Juvenile Justice to be part of the supervision order, the probation officer may be asked to provide purposeful activities for the young person placed under a supervision order.

The probation service keeps in touch with young offenders who receive a custodial sentence through officers seconded to detention and youth custody centres.

The courts can ask probation officers, acting as welfare officers, to prepare reports about such questions as the care and custody of children affected by domestic upheaval or family break up.

Through-care Work
Some probation officers work on secondment in prisons, borstals, detention centres, adult probation hostels and bail hostels. They can provide an essential link between a prisoner serving a long custodial sentence and the outside world, keeping alive family relationships and contacts with friends and employers. The work with inmates is aimed at getting them to admit responsibility for what they have done, helping them to learn from their experience and prepare for a more socially acceptable life outside the institution. Individual or group counselling may be involved.

The prison probation teams work closely with prison staff and members of specialist agencies. Normally, the period of secondment to prison work lasts about three years during which time team members maintain both professional links with their own area management and contact with probation officers in the areas where prisoners in their care will be released.

Newly released young offenders and adult prisoners on parole need supervision, and probation officers try to provide the kind of help that will ensure offenders do not go back inside; this involves putting them in touch with those statutory or voluntary bodies that can enable them to find food, clothing and possibly employment.

The Wider Role

Probation teams in some areas have set up drop-in centres. These places cater very informally for people with a range of problems, for example, the homeless, the unemployed and the dependents of someone serving a prison sentence. Some visitors to drop-in centres may be seeking no more than a cup of tea and a warm room to sit in for an hour or two, but others can benefit from some structured activity such as literacy or numeracy training.

The probation service has an important contribution to make to the new work of support for the victims of crime and of making the offender aware of the consequences of his or her antisocial behaviour. Tentative steps are being taken to arrange limited contact between victim and offender, which can sometimes lead to the offender's making reparation to the victim.

Conditions and Prospects

The Home Office, which organises the probation and after-care service in England and Wales, financially sponsors some students who obtain places on certain courses in England and Wales. The level of provision is linked to the number of jobs for trained officers expected to be available and information about sponsorship is obtainable from the Home Office (address on p 110). Sponsorship is not available to those who are 50 by the time the course begins nor to those who have restrictions on their stay of employment in the UK.

In England and Wales the ranks are as follows: main-grade probation officer, senior probation officer, assistant chief probation officer, deputy chief probation officer and chief probation officer. Promotion, which depends on merit and not on length of service, can be quite difficult to achieve. There are few opportunities for practical probation work at levels above senior probation officer. It is possible to advance to senior advisory or managerial posts. The supervisory posts are usually advertised nationally and filled from within the service. By the start of 1990 there were 1,412 such posts among some 6,936 full-time officer posts. A qualified probation officer can also get a teaching post as a tutor, training officer or student supervisor in an educational establishment or with a voluntary organisation.

Competition for posts has increased in recent years and you should be prepared to be flexible about where you work.

Much of a probation officer's work is done within normal office hours, but some evening and Saturday duties are necessary as probationers may not be available at other times. Conscientious probation officers tend to become deeply involved in their work and, sometimes, in their clients' problems; for the sake of their own mental well-being they should learn how to 'switch off' when not working. The holiday allowance is 36 days per year.

Retirement age is 65 for both men and women, but an officer with 25 reckonable years' service may retire at 60.

You can get further information on specific local points by contacting your area chief probation officer (listed in the telephone directory under Probation Service).

Case Study
Philip is a probation officer in Inner London, with ten years' experience.

You've got to be a bit of an actor, really understand how to sell the best interests of your client to the court – to the judge or magistrate. You've got to prepare reports people can understand, then speak up and make judgements about people that you can support, because what the court decides will affect their whole future. My proudest moments, and my gloomiest, come after I've made a court appearance for someone, and the magistrates either back my judgement or reject it. I find that public side of the work very challenging and stimulating, and you can't escape the responsibility of knowing what value you represent to each offender coming up for trial and sentence. I like the chance to stick my neck out for somebody and try to persuade other people to go along with it. But I like to make objective appraisals, and sometimes that means persuading the offender to go along with a course of action he or she doesn't favour. It's often slow hard work trying to get people to accept that they must improve their behaviour, especially if you feel strongly about the social conditions they live with which may make antisocial behaviour very understandable.

We form a kind of buffer between the offender and the world at large – educating each about the other. You need a thick skin to keep plugging on trying to help individuals improve themselves when often society and even they themselves think the way you work is a waste of time. We work with individuals on their personal problems – how to manage money, get and keep a job, say – and with groups, perhaps of offenders doing community service, or adult illiterates, or boys on probation learning car mechanics instead of taking and driving away. It's versatile stuff, and you need a bit of entrepreneurial flair too.

The Prison Service

England, Wales and Northern Ireland
The prison service is part of the home civil service and is administered by the Home Office. It is responsible for detaining people who have been committed to custody by the law – both those awaiting trial and those convicted after trial. The service is also responsible for developing and implementing 'constructive methods of treatment designed to lead to the prisoner's rehabilitation and reform'.

Scotland
The Secretary of State for Scotland is responsible to Parliament for the Scottish prison service and the Scottish Home and Health Department is principally involved in administering the service. The Social Welfare Department is responsible for the after-care of those who have served their sentence.

Prisons in the UK are overcrowded and many of them are old buildings in a poor state of repair, but the older establishments are not necessarily the most depressing ones to work in; the atmosphere of a penal institution depends very much on the personality of its governor and the kind of team spirit he or she has tried to build up among the officers.

There are a number of factors which contribute to making prison work stressful and you will find this whatever kind of establishment you work in. There is a rising crime rate and a shortage of prison staff; the government, in an attempt to get better value for money out of the prison service, recently introduced a scheme called 'Fresh Start' which involved the use of work practices designed, among other things, to cut down excess overtime, and some staff do not like this; prisoners are occasionally violent, hostile, disruptive or psychologically disturbed and it has to be said that the work can be dangerous; the atmosphere can be both tense and claustrophobic; and prison officers may have disagreeable duties to perform, such as supervising slopping out. On top of all this, you will have to contend with the attitude of the public towards those in law-enforcement occupations. On the one hand, people expect to be protected from the dangerous members of society, and on the other, they are quick to find fault and complain, with the result that prison staff, and members of the police force, can feel driven to spend their leisure time among those in similar employment; this sense of isolation can be compounded by the fact that they often live apart from the community in service accommodation.

The Institutions
England, Wales and Northern Ireland
Remand centres are mainly for young offenders and women who have been committed in custody for trial or sentence.

Local prisons deal with men, women and young offenders and are responsible for the intitial assessment and classification of a convicted prisoner. They offer a variety of work.

Training prisons provide work, training facilities and vocational education courses in a wide range of skills. There are 'open' and 'closed' institutions.

Young offender institutions are for offenders aged between 15 and 21 and they provide inmates with training.

Detention centres are for offenders aged between 14 and 21 who are serving shorter sentences than those sent to young offender institutions.

When you are newly appointed, you will be required to work wherever you are needed, but later in your career your wishes as regards your place of work will be given every consideration.

Scotland
In Scotland there are 14 prisons for persons over the age of 21, 13 for men and one for women, and they have the dual function of holding adults on remand and after they have been sentenced. There are two types of prison, regional and local. Of the men's institutions, one has less restrictive conditions, one is an 'open' prison and three have special facilities to accommodate prisoners 'who create very severe management problems', potentially violent prisoners or those who 'for whatever reason would

benefit from a period away from the main prison'. There are young offender institutions (including two 'open') for young male offenders aged between 16 and 21, one detention centre and one remand institution accommodating youths under 21.

Organisation and Prospects

A *governor* is responsible for all staff and inmates and for the efficient working of every aspect of the institution under his/her control. Many governors started their careers as prison officers, but there is an open entry competition for assistant governor (trainee) posts. There are four classes of governor and opportunities for promotion above governor class to assistant controller and director.

The *assistant governor's* work is essentially managerial.

There are four classes of *prison officer*; after two years' service prison officers may take the examination to qualify for promotion to assistant governor (trainee). Under 'Fresh Start' it is necessary to have officers achieve senior grades in their 40s. For those officers considered suitable, this will mean accelerated promotion through the ranks every two to four years. The most senior uniformed officer, the chief officer, keeps the governor informed on the day-to-day happenings and activities, maintains discipline and controls the work of the other officers. There is a separate career path and good promotion prospects for trades officers and other specialists.

The Work

It is possible only to give a general idea of the work, because institutions and their inmates vary so widely. The regime of a landing officer in a high security prison will be very different from that of an officer in an open prison.

The governor's work is essentially administrative and involves carrying out regular tours of inspection. The assistant governor, who may be in charge of a wing or a unit in a young offender institution or detention centre, works with outside specialists, such as medical and welfare officers, and may be responsible for staff training. He or she will sometimes deputise for the governor at meetings and is expected to know the inmates.

The main duty of prison officers is the secure detention of prisoners and this involves patrolling buildings and grounds, searching cells and doing surveillance duty on landings. There is also reception and classification duty, and general supervision of work done by inmates. Officers in a local prison spend quite a lot of time escorting prisoners to and from court and to other prisons. The work is varied and demanding; if you are interested in people and willing to get involved, you can do a great deal to help prisoners. In certain kinds of institution officers mix informally with inmates and, by establishing rapport, can become a stabilising influence in their lives. Many prisoners are deeply inadequate people lacking the most basic social skills; officers can help such people acquire some of these skills and so prepare themselves for life outside. There are, of course, ruthless, hardened criminals in prison and from time to time you will have to be firm and assertive, and will need the resilience to cope with abuse and violence. As a prison officer you will be expected to work as a member of a team and it is possible that you will not be in sympathy with all your colleagues. Above all you need to be flexible, mature and have a balanced approach to life.

Specialist Work
Bricklayers, carpenters, electricians, painters and plumbers can work in prisons as trades officers, who, after three years' service, can qualify by examination for promotion through works officer grades, to become chief officer (works).There are few trades officer posts for women. If you have successfully completed a recognised training for other trades, eg tailoring or dressmaking, laundry work, wood machining, metal work or engineering, you could be appointed an officer instructor to teach your skills and run a prison workshop.

Officers with or without previous experience, who show suitability, can apply to train as caterers or physical education instructors.

The prison nursing service welcomes those with qualifications/experience or interest in nursing the physically or mentally sick to train as hospital officers or join the prison nursing service.

Entry Requirements
There are no minimum educational qualifications required for the prison service, though a high standard of education is expected of candidates for assistant governors' and governors' posts. Two-thirds of all recruits hold degrees or diplomas or have had experience or training in social studies, institutional management or law. You must fulfil the following basic conditions:

☐ You must be aged between 21 and 49½ (England, Wales, Northern Ireland), or between 20 and 42 with an extension if you have had long service in the armed forces (Scotland).

☐ If you are a woman you must be at least 160cm in height, if a man, at least 167.7cm (England, Wales, Northern Ireland) or 170cm (Scotland).

☐ You should be able to provide good references.

☐ You must give details of any convictions (but an offence is not an automatic bar to selection).

☐ You must be a British citizen, or a British protected person, or a citizen of the Irish Republic, or, subject to certain conditions, a Commonwealth citizen.

☐ In order to qualify for interview you must pass an aptitude test.

☐ You must have good general health and good eyesight, although spectacles or contact lenses are not necessarily a bar. You must be prepared to have a full medical examination.

Training
England, Wales and Northern Ireland
Before you begin your formal training you will spend two weeks in a penal establishment getting to know prison functions and observing experienced officers at work. Formal training begins with a nine-week residential course at one of the officer training schools which combines classroom learning with practical exercises. You will also learn first aid, physical restraint, self defence techniques and inter-personal skills.

After your first posting you will receive on-the-job training and you will be able to attend regional refresher and development courses throughout your career.

Officers can be sponsored to do educational courses where the service will pay the majority of the fees and allow study leave.

Scotland
You will spend your first two weeks at a penal establishment working closely with experienced officers who will introduce you to various aspects of prison life. Then you will go on a six-week residential course at the Prison Service College. There you will receive instruction on security, prisoner classification, escorts, supervision and party control; you will attend lectures on the structure of the service, the treatment of prisoners, problems of reform, training and principles of leadership; you will learn

control and restraint techniques, and first aid; and you will visit other establishments. Your first 12 months after appointment will be probationary.

Assistant Governor (Trainee)
There is direct entry to assistant governor (trainee) posts via a civil service open competition. Successful candidates serve a two-year probationary period during which time they attend short residential courses at the Prison Service College and receive supervised on-the-job training. Trainees are also seconded to allied services and, if they have not served as prison officers, follow courses at the Officers' Training School.

Conditions of Work
When you are appointed as a prison officer you may be posted to work in any penal establishment (appropriate to your sex) but in England, Wales and Northern Ireland consideration will be given to your circumstances and wishes when your posting is being decided. Scottish prison officers remain liable throughout their career to serve in any establishment in Scotland. When you have successfully completed 12 months' service your appointment will be confirmed. You may retire at the age of 60 with a pension and a lump sum related to your length of service.

You will work a 39–41 hour (39-hour in Scotland), five-day week with extra payment for overtime and weekend duties. Night duty is not frequent. Holiday entitlement begins with four weeks and two days per year and goes up to six weeks after 25 years' total service.

You will receive either a housing allowance or, when available, you will be offered free service accommodation (a self-contained flat or house). Prison officers wear uniform, which is provided, and receive a shoe allowance.

The National Association for the Care and Resettlement of Offenders (NACRO)

NACRO is a registered charity, a company limited by guarantee and a registered housing association. Most of its community projects are carried out by NACRO Community Enterprises (NCE) Ltd, a wholly owned subsidiary. NACRO employs about 1,000 staff on over 100 projects and other services in England and Wales and works closely with other national and local agencies, and with local communities. Scotland has a completely separate, much smaller, organisation, the Scottish Association for the Care and Resettlement of Offenders (SACRO). All NACRO's work is devoted to developing more humane and effective ways of dealing with crime; it promotes the care and resettlement of offenders in the community, helps the victims of crime and involves the community in crime prevention. Its projects are used voluntarily and are not part of any court order.

The Projects
Services for Offenders and Others
These services are in the fields of housing, education and training, employment, youth training (see *Careers Working with Children and Young People*), prison links and resettlement, court-based services and welfare. They are intended to help offenders (or those who might be drawn into crime) keep out of trouble by providing practical help, for example, accommodation in hostels and self-contained flats, education and training at education activity centres, running Youth Training and Community Programme schemes, and working alongside probation officers to offer alternatives to prison.

Tackling Crime in the Community
Run-down residential areas display a range of serious social problems and lack communal facilities. NACRO's Crime Prevention Unit works with residents, local authority departments and other agencies, develops action plans and monitors the effects of improvements as they are brought about. The Neighbourhood Activities Units work with local communities and agencies to develop constructive activities for children and young people who are at risk of offending. The projects they set up are funded for a maximum of 36 months, at the end of which time most of them should be able to continue on their own.

Making Things Happen
The rest of NACRO's work is concerned mainly with developing better ways of working with offenders and tackling crime. There is a Juvenile Crime Section, which provides information, monitoring and development services to local authorities and other organisations, a Black Initiatives Unit, a Training Team, a Research Unit and an Information Department.

Working with NACRO

NACRO does not have a 'career structure'. Its staff do not have to have social work qualifications, but are recruited on the strength of their personal qualities, skills and experience. Newly recruited personnel are given on-the-job training and attend short training courses. Promotion can be rapid; you can be given responsibility young. Many staff are working on short-term contracts and certain posts are open only to long-term unemployed people.

Case Study

Nigel is a senior consultant worker with a Neighbourhood Development Unit.

I got a job with NACRO by sheer chance. I'd been on the dole for three-and-a-half years and my dad manages another scheme; he talked to a few people and got me fixed up with an interview. I went along and luckily got a job.

When I started, I was doing stuff that was linked with surveying which I'd done at school. I went through statistics, which I could do anyway, and I went on a few training courses down in London and gradually learned the ropes.

I've been setting up a residents' association on a council estate. The people we're working with are the normal people you'd find on any council estate; there are a lot of single-parent families and many of the people are from ethnic minority groups. This is a post-survey project; we surveyed the area and a colleague of mine decided there was a need for a residents' association. I went along with that and we ran a series of meetings with the residents to see how they felt about a residents' association specifically to set up certain facilities on the estate. This was an estate with nothing on it at all, no facilities of any kind, but there was this derelict building in the middle of it and we decided to push for that and try to get something going there with the Council. The Council had told us that we'd need to get a residents' association going to give us a bit more clout. We had to arrange a meeting and so we went round knocking on doors to get people to come to a meeting. It took three meetings in all, from the initial telling them what was going to happen and what we were aiming for, to the actual forming of the residents' association and getting the constitution drawn up. Now we've started fund-raising events; there's a car-boot sale coming up, which they've organised. The idea is to get them established, with our support – we've got the Council's support as well – for the first year and then we're going to pull out and the thing should run itself.

The other thing I got involved in was adult literacy. To begin with I picked up most of it as I went along, from experience of doing the job. Then, earlier this year, I went on an in-service training course. I work in conjunction with ALBSU, the Adult Literacy and Basic Skills Unit; they do the advertising and set up the groups and I'm a volunteer tutor. I'm on a course at the moment for literacy - for an ABE, Adult Basic Education, Certificate - and we're hoping in the new year to set up an in-house literacy scheme just for people on the NACRO Community Programme.

The major thing we have to do is build up self-confidence and we try to create an informal atmosphere so the students can enjoy it. We use the basic ALBSU teaching techniques and we use the computer - there's computer software. I deal with a very wide range of people of all abilities and from all walks of life. What you do with them depends a lot on their level and what they want to gain from it. Some of them just want to learn to read, but we tend to push them towards writing as well, others only need to polish up on the odd bit of spelling and that sort of thing. Most of the teaching has been one-to-one. ALBSU closed down through the summer, but we decided to carry on with a tutor from ALBSU because we didn't think it was fair on the students to break. Now, we're moving towards group work and we've got a fairly strong group on both days.

I really enjoy the literacy work. A few years ago, when I was in the sixth form, I did think about teaching; the only thing that held me back was that I doubted whether I'd be any good at it. But through NACRO - which was pure hit or miss, it was a case of them needing a volunteer tutor and me coming along - I found I was reasonable at it. I hope that in five years' time or so I shall be teaching. I've applied for a place at teacher training college this year and my NACRO experience has been invaluable; it has given me a teaching qualification which stands me in good stead to move on to teacher training college and there's a possibility that the amount of hours I've done with ALBSU will cut down my third vocational year.

Juvenile Justice Work

Juvenile Justice work, previously known as Intermediate Treatment, is an attempt to reduce delinquency in children and young people aged between 7 and 17 (see *Careers Working With Children and Young People*). Most local authorities have Juvenile Justice services but they are often provided in partnership with voluntary agencies and the education or probation service. The kinds of children referred to schemes are those who are suffering from the effects of poor family relationships and are perhaps lacking in positive adult attention and are consequently unmotivated and unable to relieve their own boredom and frustration. Many regularly play truant, start to underachieve, become disruptive and then begin to offend, resulting in convictions. There are two kinds of work in Juvenile Justice, full-time and sessional.

Chapter 6

Counselling and Advice Work

Counselling

The word 'counselling' crops up frequently in connection with social work; social workers, health visitors, probation and education welfare officers all counsel their clients. So too, of course, do teachers, doctors, religious leaders, psychotherapists and many other professionals. What is counselling? It is most emphatically not telling people what to do. The British Association for Counselling (BAC) describes it as 'giving the client an opportunity to explore, discover and clarify ways of living more resourcefully and towards greater well-being'. In other words, counsellors help clients to help themselves.

Counselling usually lasts for only a few sessions, though it can continue for several months, but if it is to be successful a trusting relationship has to be built up between counsellor and client. The counsellor listens carefully, sympathetically and respectfully, without offering judgement, and encourages the client to express feelings such as anger, grief or anxiety which may have become bottled up. Training enables counsellors to help a client release powerful emotions without themselves becoming burdened by them; training also makes them self-aware and provides them with a repertoire of skills and an understanding of their theoretical basis.

Some counsellors specialise in particular areas, eg drug dependency or group work. There is no clear dividing line between counselling and psychotherapy. Counselling is usually less formal and continues over a shorter period than psychotherapy, but there is a lot of overlap between the two activities.

Although there are recognised training courses for counsellors (see pp 105-7), few people, after qualifying and perhaps becoming accredited by the BAC, immediately begin doing full-time counselling; most combine it with other related work and gradually take on more clients as their skills develop and reputation builds up. Counsellors work in schools, colleges, polytechnics and universities, in industry, in GPs' practices, in welfare and voluntary organisations and in private practice.

Case Study
John is senior counsellor in a university counselling service.

I came in to my present job through a circuitous route: in my forties I decided I needed a life change; I'd been a marriage guidance counsellor for 12 years and it seemed a natural progression to move into full-time counselling. A job happened to come up in the city where I was working, I applied and got it on the basis of my experience and training. I gave up my job in the prison service and began working as a full-time counsellor in a college of further education. After six years, during which time I did a three-year, part-time diploma course in student counselling, I saw a university post advertised. I've been in this job for nine years; after being here for three years my colleague retired and I took over as senior counsellor.

About two-thirds of our clients are undergraduates, that is, people doing their first degree, and one-third are postgraduate. We also see members of the teaching staff; they pay for the service, whereas the students are paid for out of their college capitation. The kinds of problems that clients consult us about can very roughly be divided into three areas: first, the business of separating themselves from their background and from home and parents; second, problems of personal identify – who am I?; and third, work-related problems, which very often turn out to be mainly problems of study management. We see 80 per cent of the people between once and ten times, so most of the work is short-term, focused work. People come with a problem, we'll try and focus on it; we see whether that problem can be shifted and whether there are any other problems that need to be focused on, and, if there are, whether they have to be dealt with now or can wait. On the whole, if they can wait, we would encourage the student to deal with them themselves at some other time and in some other place; if they can't, of course, we've got to engage with them, so the other 20 per cent of our clients we work with long term. Every new student is leafleted. We've been around quite a few years and we've got a good reputation. We get referrals from tutors, medical services, psychiatric services and clergy. Some students are referred by their peers; people say: 'Why don't you go to the counselling service, they're confidential and professional?'

We are staffed by some full-time and some part-time staff and we use volunteers. Psychotherapists and counsellors in training need experience and placements and in return for a few weekly sessions from them we give work supervision and some in-service training.

This enables us to meet the fairly terrific need that we cope with. It is also refreshing and stimulating for us to have new people coming in to work with us all the time; they have new ideas and look at things in different ways. It is very important for us to keep our own minds stimulated, to be continually doing in-service training. We have regular case discussions, regular sessions with a consultant psychotherapist and we are all in therapy ourselves. If you're going to be a counsellor or psychotherapist you need to look at your own motivations, at what's going on in your own life, at your own feelings, because all the time these are being engaged by your clients and if you're not clear about who you are and where you're at and what you're on about, you're in danger of spilling over into them or of letting them spill over into you, and once those boundaries begin to crumble it's difficult to do any effective work. We also arrange our own outside supervision, so one way or another we ensure that we get adequate supervision urselves. You sometimes work with people who are very depressed, suicidal or disturbed, so you need to be able to stand back and reflect about the way you're relating to them and the sort of things you say to them and how you respond to what they say to you; it's pretty essential to have an outsider to help you conceptualise the process.

Counselling is an attractive-sounding task and a lot of people, when they identify that they are interested in people, often think counselling is what they'd like to do. One has to emphasise, however, that it is an extremely demanding job because you are meeting disturbed and needy people. You must have your own feet firmly on the ground and understand your own internal world, your own problems and your own relationships, and be prepared to work across the very difficult boundary that exists between the external world of fact and activity and the internal world of fantasy, anxiety and memory. The fascinating thing about counselling is that you get to know people very intimately, very quickly, but that has its dangers. People put themselves into your hands, into your care, and you have to be very careful for them and careful of the boundaries. It is important to be absolutely professional. There are too many people out there who are not qualified and not experienced; they are setting themselves up as counsellors and they don't have very much idea about boundaries. Clients are very vulnerable when they're crying and telling you how awful they feel and of course they need emotional arms around them and obviously it's not much of a step to put physical arms around them as well, but it's usually very important not to do that. What we're doing as counsellors is helping people to put their own arms around themselves. Counsellors have to be involved with their clients but separate from them; we do not talk about ourselves - although one may answer the odd direct question - what we do is to focus on the clients and get them to talk about themselves and in that way we help them learn to stand on their own feet and manage their own lives.

Marriage Guidance (Relate)

Relate, the country's largest marital and personal counselling agency, employs only a few salaried staff who coordinate its work and provide specialist support and advisory services. Most of its 1,700 trained counsellors work on a part-time, voluntary basis. However, a fairly detailed account of Relate's work is included in this book because the training provided by Relate and experience of marriage guidance counselling would be very useful to anyone who has embarked upon, or is thinking of taking up, social work.

Relate itself is a limited company and registered charity consisting of one representative from each of the 160 constituent local Relate centres in England, Wales and Northern Ireland (Scotland has its own service); its affairs are managed by an elected executive committee. Funding comes from a Home Office grant, other grants and donations, from the sale of publications and from the provision of training facilities for other organisations.

Local centres are independent bodies managed by their own executive committees and they vary a good deal. They are funded from a number of sources, but most obtain about half their income from local authority grants. They used to depend entirely upon voluntary workers but most centres now employ a number of salaried full- or part-time receptionists or office managers and some pay counsellors for work done over and above their minimum voluntary commitment of 120 hours per year. The counselling service is free but clients are asked to make a contribution.

Selection of Counsellors

Relate is an independent body, not attached to any sectarian, denominational or cultural institution. Its members are not required to assent to any dogma or beliefs and in practice are drawn from all creeds and none. Counsellors are expected to recognise the value and dignity of every human being irrespective of origin, status, sex, sexual orientation, age, belief or contribution to society.

The initial recruitment of counsellors is done by local Relate centres, the sponsoring committee of which decides whether or not applicants are suitable to be sent for selection for training. Candidates who get through the initial stage attend a one-day selection conference, where they are interviewed by a marriage guidance tutor and an external selector working in a related field. On the basis of this interview and a number of personality tests and group discussions, about half the applicants are accepted for training, details of which are given on p 107.

The Work
Marriage Guidance Counselling
There are some 400 Relate centres in England, Wales and Northern Ireland which handle about 40,000 new cases every year. Counselling is available to anyone; some clients come because they have been referred by a doctor or clergyman, but most have been told about the service by someone who has used it or have been advised by their families to seek help from the organisation.

A counsellor's first tasks are to make his or her clients feel relaxed and at ease, because it is hard to pour out your most intimate problems to a complete stranger, and to assure them of the absolute confidentiality of the service. Sessions last for an hour a week and counselling will continue for as long as is necessary – on average five to six weeks. The most important part of the work is listening, actively listening, reflecting back to people what they are saying, checking out with them what they really mean. Sometimes an experienced counsellor will set 'homework' tasks; for example, if a husband and wife cannot talk to each other, they might be encouraged to sit down for 20 minutes in the evening, with the television switched off, and just talk. When clients have been referred, eg by a doctor, counsellors will contact the doctor to say whether or not they have taken on the client and at the end of the counselling will let him or her know that it has been completed. Every counsellor commits him or herself to 120 hours' work per year, which in practice means seeing, on average, three sets of clients a week. More time will be needed for writing up case notes and for doing the necessary reading and study, and there are fortnightly case discussion groups to attend. Follow-up studies show that about half the clients are well satisfied with the service and enjoy improved family relationships, and a further quarter report some improvement.

Case Study
Sylvia is a marriage guidance counsellor.

I had thought about doing the work for a long time, because I seemed to have a lot of people talk to me about their marriages going wrong and I wanted to be able to help them in a more effective way, so I took the training. Once you are trained, things are set up for you by the local office. The secretary has a waiting list of people who need to see a counsellor and when you've done sufficient training, your tutor will say, 'Now you can start. You can have two sets of clients.'

Deciding to see a marriage guidance counsellor is a very difficult step for someone to take and I admire our clients very much. They come along to a strange room and see a strange man or woman and pour out their most intimate problems and it's very difficult for them, so the biggest job we have at this stage is to make them feel comfortable. That's part of the early training, you're taught how to sit in a room with them and basic things like how to arrange the chairs. You can learn a lot about a couple from the way they're sitting in their chairs - that's another part of the training. Are they all knotted up? Are their arms tightly folded, their legs crossed? Are they turning away from each other? Sometimes they can't look at each other, sometimes they can only look at you and say to you what they have been dying to say to their partner for a long time but haven't been able to.

People with problems often go to their families first, but families, even with the best will in the world, take sides and the thing about a counsellor - particularly when the couple come together - is that you're completely neutral and you're hearing both sides. You're able to show one partner what the other is saying. You ask, 'Did you hear what he said?' 'What did you hear her say?' And they repeat it and it can be quite different from what the person actually said. Listening is the most important part. You intervene with things like, 'Are you saying so and so?' and very often they say 'No, I'm saying something different' and that way you make them think about what they're saying. We all tend to exaggerate problems when we do not spell them out. People will go away from the first interview and find they have already moved a long way. The fact that they have come in the first place means that they want change. Of course, it can be very painful; we get a lot of tears in the counselling room - there's a lot of pain around. When two people have taken the decision to come they really want it to work, as opposed to the wife who brings her husband along to be 'changed', or the husband who wants his wife 'put right' or 'told off'. Then it's up to the counsellor to show them what they're doing.

I think it's terribly important to remember that there isn't a standard for marriage. Two people decide what is right for them in their marriage and although the counsellor may think, 'That wouldn't work for me, I couldn't live in a marriage like that', you must always remember that it's the clients' marriage you are talking about, not yours. If you can help them just to shift one tiny bit, it might make it very tolerable for them, although for another couple it might not be okay.

You actually see when you're successful, you can see it happening in the room, because over the weeks the couple will change. The way they dress will change slightly, the way they sit will change, they might come in holding hands one day. Gradually, instead of being a three, with the couple talking to you, they talk more and more to each other and you are almost observing. Then you know it's working; they're taking back responsibility themselves for what they're doing and they'll check out now and again with you. We do have lovely letters from people and people will ring in or they'll send you a Christmas card.

The work is not paid and many people go on after about six years to other things. I've now become a tutor. I still have to fulfil my minimum 120 hours' counselling a year, but I've done further training so that I can help other counsellors in their work. Help them by doing some teaching, supervising their work, help them to make the most of their two years' training, help them by picking up on the points where they have had a problem, encourage them to do more training, to go back for further days. Sometimes you encourage people to take up another form of work within marriage guidance - educational work, going into schools or running groups inside prisons. There is a lot of allied work and I encourage counsellors who are fully trained perhaps to do this.

Marital Sexual Therapy (MST)

There are now 120 counsellors who have received additional training in MST (see p 107) and therapy is offered at 68 centres. What is treated is sexual dysfunction (eg male impotence or female orgasmic problems) and a couple must have a good general relationship before they are accepted for MST. They come for an hour's session per week and therapy lasts on average four to five months. Before therapy can begin the therapist sees the couple together and separately and takes a detailed history which enables him or her to assess whether or not clients are suitable for, and will benefit from, therapy. If, for example, a couple are quarrelling violently their sexual relations are likely to be poor and they will probably be referred for counselling rather than MST.

Much MST is educational - many sexual problems stem from ignorance - and with the aid of clear diagrams and photographs a husband and wife will be taught about their own and their partner's body. No exercises are performed in the counselling room, but clients are set tasks to perform at home and the results are discussed with the therapist. Gradually, by simple stages, they learn about arousal and excitement. Follow-up studies show that 60 per cent of clients achieve and maintain an enhanced level of sexual performance.

Case Study
Rose is a marital sexual therapist.

The work is essentially with couples and it is marital work. We see the couple together for the first session and we do an assessment, then we see them individually and take a very, very detailed history. A history of their childhood, first sexual experience, first kiss, first boyfriend, what it was like for a girl when she started her periods, what this relationship is like, if there has been another marriage, if they have children, what it was like having the children, what hobbies they have – a very, very detailed history. Your training enables you to see a pattern emerging, it teaches you how to pick things out. When you've done the histories and decided that the couple could benefit from MST you spend a lot of time planning how you're going to help them.

I think it must be hard for people to seek help, though some people find it easier to come with a physical problem than with a relationship problem. Sometimes a problem appears to be a physical problem, for example impotence, but it becomes clear when you've done the assessment that it's a counselling problem. Maybe the husband dislikes his wife intensely and this is the only way he can tell her, then you have to try to persuade the couple to go for marriage guidance counselling. Sometimes they'll accept this, sometimes they won't. MST is what they came for and they won't accept that there's a problem in the marriage.

Therapy takes up to 20 weeks. In the counselling room it's talk only, they don't do any exercises there, but you set them things to do at home, certain things to do three times a week, to try out; we call it 'homework'. You start by helping them get used to touching each other's body, that's the first stage. You step up gradually, by very small stages, this 'pleasuring' until they begin to understand what excites them and what excites their partner. The next time, you ask them how they got on and you write down what they tell you. Then you can look back and say, 'Six weeks ago you couldn't do that and now you can.' Usually, it's extremely successful, it works very well.

People's sexual expectations are much higher nowadays because there's so much frank and explicit writing about sex. A lot of our work is making sure that what our clients want is real and not something they have read about in a magazine. It has got to be something that is right for them. A great deal of MST is educational work; there is sex education now and sex is talked about a lot, but we have to fill in the gaps. Paradoxically, the more sex is talked about the fewer real facts people have, because they feel they 'ought' to know and don't like to ask.

Education and Training
Every year counsellors and education workers devote 15,000 hours to educational work, most of it carried out in small discussion groups. They work with young people in schools and youth clubs, parents in antenatal clinics, engaged couples, parents of handicapped children and prisoners. Relate tutors and counsellors provide training sessions for social workers, teachers, clergy, personnel officers, health service employees and other groups concerned with social welfare.

Psychotherapy

The term psychotherapy covers a range of therapies. A psychotherapist uses psychological methods to relieve emotional distress or to help clients change certain attitudes or aspects of their behaviour. Treatment is usually more intense and longer drawn out than counselling, eg it can take place as often as five times a week and continue over several years. There are a number of different schools of psychotherapy; if you are interested in the subject but know nothing about it, send for MIND's factsheet on talking treatments (enclosing a stamped, addressed envelope).

The Citizens' Advice Bureau

Citizens' Advice Bureaux (CABx) give free, confidential and impartial advice to all who approach them and try 'to ensure that individuals do not suffer through ignorance of their rights and responsibilities or of the services available, or through an inability to express their needs effectively'. There are 900 CABx in the UK; one post in ten is a paid post, but 90 per cent of the 15,000 trained advisers are voluntary workers. In addition, local professional people, such as accountants, solicitors, architects and surveyors, provide free advice sessions.

Each local bureau is autonomous and, while having access to a national information system that is centrally prepared and updated each month, is geared to cater for local needs. People seek advice from CABx on all sorts of matters, but the 'top six enquiries' concern social security, consumer/debt/money matters, housing/homelessness, family/personal matters, employment/redundancy and justice. Two areas in which CABx are doing an increasing amount of work are tribunal assistance and representation at county courts, and debt counselling. If a CAB cannot provide the help or expertise a client needs it will, with the client's agreement, refer him or her to a specialised agency for further information or action, when necessary making the appointment and sending a person to accompany the client.

CAB staff are as varied in age, background and character as their clients, but all are mature, committed people with a professional attitude to their work. One of the first things they have to learn is how to interview; this involves listening, giving the client time to explain the problem and then asking questions to clarify the issues. Giving information involves finding your way round the bureau's files and reference books, and knowing what other specialist agencies exist. Giving advice is not a matter of telling clients what to do but of describing the options that are open in order that they can decide what is the most suitable course of action. Practical help includes drafting letters, making telephone calls, filling in forms, making quite complicated calculations to work out benefits or tax, mediating in conflicts and representing clients at tribunals. All cases are recorded to enable the bureau to offer an efficient service if the client returns. There is a certain amount of basic office administration, such as updating files, checking stocks of leaflets and typing letters, which is usually done by the paid staff.

If you think you would enjoy and might be suitable for the work, contact your local CAB, which will be listed in the telephone directory. A full list of CABx is given in the *Social Services Year Book* and the *Charities Digest*, both of which are kept in local reference libraries. You will be given an application form on which you are asked to supply quite detailed information about yourself and during the initial interview, which will last about an hour, you will have the chance to ask questions. After successfully completing a basic training course, which will include visits to the DHSS, courts and a Jobcentre, and involve doing written homework, you can begin working at the bureau under supervision. You will also receive on-the-job training from your bureau colleagues, attend regular training sessions and have the chance to go to further training courses from time to time.

Case Study
Anna recently trained as a volunteer; her account, published in a local bureau's annual report, is reproduced with permission.

'What feelings did you have on arrival here this morning?' asked the training course co-ordinator, after we had all made our introductions. Probably the most truthful answer to this would have been the conditioned fear of school – several strange faces, a rather soulless 'classroom' and the promise of 'case studies', 'exercises' and even 'homework'!

Even if the nine-week whistle-stop tour of benefits, housing, the legal system, debt, etc, did resemble school just a little, it was nevertheless great fun. The tutors somehow managed to sustain the interest of a diverse group of ages and backgrounds. This can't have been easy since the group included a retired water engineer, several mothers with young children, a businesswoman, three unemployed people and myself, a research student in oriental languages. By the end of the course we were a friendly lot, expressing our opinions openly and just a touch concerned that any information we had acquired was the tip of a rather large iceberg.

The next week was straight down to business at the Bureau. An apprehensive and nervous start, especially on the telephone; I felt rather more exposed up here than previously downstairs on the reception desk, where I had spent part of my training. On reception I could cheerfully pass the calls on!

The first face-to-face interview – a single parent debt problem – seemed a bit easier, things went more at my pace. What struck me then, as indeed now, was the confidence the client places in you as a worker. In spite of my being fairly young, people of all ages and both sexes actually trust me to help them! Sometimes the feeling of responsibility for that trust makes me want to do more than I actually can – but if I feel dissatisfied there's always 'one of the team' I can moan to.

It's been a stimulating and happy first year at the CAB; I hope I shall have many more.

The Samaritans

There are 182 Samaritan branches throughout the country providing a 24-hour confidential listening and befriending service. All workers are volunteers; they are ordinary people of all ages and backgrounds and the only things they have in common are human warmth and a desire to help those in distress.

Some clients come to a Samaritan branch, which is usually open from 9.00am till 10.30pm, a few write, but the great majority phone in. Many callers are in a very distressed state and a volunteer's first task is to listen and reassure. Some people's problems blow up very quickly, tempting them to act impulsively, and a single telephone conversation may be enough to stop a person trying to commit suicide. Other people have problems, such as loneliness, guilt, marital breakdown, that have built up over a long period and these people need counselling and befriending. Samaritan volunteers are not professionals and do not offer any kind of advice or therapy; however, if a client so wishes, they can put him/her in touch with expert help.

If you would like to find out more about becoming a volunteer, contact your nearest branch which will be listed in the telephone directory. There is a thorough selection process and training programme designed to let you and the Samaritans discover if you would make a volunteer. The work is rewarding but can be very stressful; however, you can count on plenty of support from colleagues and branch organisers.

Chapter 7

Salaried Work with Charities and Voluntary Agencies

Charities and voluntary agencies cater for a very wide range of clients who have problems of a social nature – the physically disabled, the blind and partially sighted, the deaf and hard of hearing, those suffering from mental illness or mental handicap, the homeless, ethnic minorities, children and the elderly – and many of them employ full-time salaried staff, some of whom hold professional qualifications. There are posts for social workers, counsellors, occupational therapists, health visitors, teachers (with special training) and residential and day-care staff. In addition, these bodies employ administrators, information officers, publications staff, office workers and fund raisers, and they all depend a great deal upon the efforts of volunteers.

Some voluntary organisations act as agents for statutory services and, in return, receive payment for the service given; others try to reach those for whom there is no provision of any kind. There are new organisations and long-established ones, large ones with a strong administration and secure funding, and small, precarious bodies.

If you decide to work for a charity or voluntary agency you will be expected to be in sympathy with its aims and underlying values. For example, one of the conditions of employment might be that you were a practising Christian. People who do any kind of social work tend to be committed; those who do social work for a charity or voluntary organisation have to be that much more so. Back-up services and office equipment are often minimal, and premises cramped and uncomfortable. Some bodies, especially the small ones, expect all staff to muck in and perform tasks that, in a very structured set-up, would be done by office juniors. You may have to type (with two fingers?), stamp and post your own letters, not to mention making coffee and washing up the mugs.

There is no nationally agreed salary scale for qualified employees and salaries paid by charities and voluntary agencies are often lower than those in the public or private sectors; furthermore, staff may not always receive an annual pay increase. Before you accept a job, find out about such matters as pension contributions, sick and maternity leave and pay, redundancy arrangements and rights to union membership.

The large organisations are the ones that will offer the best promotion prospects. If you work for a very small outfit you will probably have to change employers in order to advance your career.

If you like the idea of doing social (in its broadest sense) work, but do not want to be swallowed up in a large bureaucratic machine or to have your hands tied by red tape, a post in the voluntary sector might be just the right thing for you. You can find out about the UK charities and voluntary organisations by consulting *The Social Services Year Book*, the *Charities Digest* and the *Voluntary Agencies Directory*, copies of which will be held by most public libraries. Write on spec to those bodies whose work area interests you and read the job advertisements in *The Guardian* (Wednesdays), *Community Care, Social Work Today* and in the minority press (eg *Asian Times, Jewish Chronicle*).

Case Study
Les does research for Shelter, the housing organisation.

Shelter has two clear tasks: as a charity it aims to raise money to provide help for those in housing need, and as a campaigning body it sets out to inform and to involve people in seeking a better deal for the homeless and badly housed. There are 10 regional centres and 35 housing aid centres that deal with inquiries from those with housing problems. Shelter has initiated and pursues a range of projects, such as the Empty Property Unit, formed to bring empty property back into use, and First Key, a support service for young people leaving local authority care and in danger of becoming homeless.

I went into Shelter at the age of 29, which is quite late - most people start earlier than that - at a time when the organisation was undergoing considerable change. I started off as a housing aid worker. I was interested in that kind of work because I had had experience of bad private landlords and had done some work to familiarise myself with the laws concerning landlord and tenant. It has now become more difficult to get into that kind of job unless you have considerable amounts of experience or a better educational background than mine - I left school at 17 and went through a variety of jobs.

Social agencies like Shelter are aware that they can easily get out of touch with the people whose interests they are trying to serve.

Increasingly, they are adopting equal opportunities policies and, in staffing terms as well as in terms of the range of issues they tackle, they are attempting to be much more reflective on the wide range of groups in our society. When I joined Shelter you could do less to help people than you can now, because the Housing and Homeless Persons Act was introduced only in 1977 after considerable pressure from Shelter and other organisations. But now the housing crisis has become so great that it is very difficult to make the rights that people have under that Act mean anything like getting a decent place to live in.

I did housing aid work for about five years. It is a very demanding job, and, although there are notable exceptions, most housing aid workers tend to need a move into another kind of work after about five years. It's like being a case worker in the social services; the caseload is far too large and the pressures on you reduce your capacity to carry out the job effectively.

I stepped sideways into a research job. Research in Shelter's terms is a mixture of researching a subject and campaigning with other organisations and groups to make the case for change in the law, in procedures and to have an effect on public attitudes if you can. Therefore, it involves contact with journalists, letters to newspapers, articles, press releases, contact with MPs, seeking to influence government bills, general lobbying, providing background briefings and, most importantly, enabling and empowering tenants' groups to have an impact on events. A researcher has to be a jack of all trades and it certainly does help if you have had some experience of housing aid work because when you're talking about an issue in global terms, you have some idea of what it means to an individual.

The work is very challenging, there are many opportunities as well as disappointments and I have always considered it a great privilege to have had the opportunity to work for Shelter. It is, in my view, a great force for good in our society, but the task ahead of it is enormous.

Part 2

Introduction

There is no simple training formula for many of the jobs described in this book and there are often several routes which can be taken to the same job. However, certain factors crop up again and again. Entry requirements to many courses include work experience; academic entry requirements to the same course may vary from college to college or may, in the case of suitably experienced mature students, be waived.

Applying for a Place

A number of courses in this field of work are full-time and run by colleges of further education, but you will find courses offered on a day-release, block-release, sandwich and second-chance basis. Courses at colleges of further education begin in September, unless otherwise stated, and applications for a place should be made direct to the college of your choice at least 10 months before you wish to begin your studies.

Most of the course are run by institutions of higher education. Admissions to polytechnics and universities (for first degree courses) are handled respectively by the Polytechnics Central Admissions System and the Universities Central Council on Admissions (see Useful Addresses, p 109). You can list up to four polytechnics and five universities in order of preference and you should apply a year in advance. A single system for polytechnic and university admissions will apply for students entering courses in 1994 with the merger of the two above bodies. Applications to study for a higher degree should be made direct to the institutions concerned.

Where there are special application procedures, these have been set out separately.

Sources of Finance

Various kinds of grant are available from local education authorities (LEAs) in England and Wales or from the education authorities or Scottish Education Department in Scotland. You should enquire locally about these. For additional information, contact the NUS (see Useful Addresses, p 109). Students embarking on postgraduate study may apply for grants to certain government departments, the Research Council and other agencies. You can get further information from the Department of Education and Science, Honeypot Lane, Canons Park, Stanmore, Middlesex, or from the Scottish Education Department, Awards Branch, Haymarket House, Clifton Terrace, Edinburgh EH12 5DT. The Department of Social Security or Scottish Education Department may offer grants for postgraduate courses in social work. If you are taking a course as on-the-job training, you will continue to receive your salary while studying. If you want to take the course through a sponsorship scheme, you must first be accepted by the authority running the scheme and then you will be told what the application procedure is. You will be paid according to a set salary scale during your training.

CCETSW candidates resident in Northern Ireland should contact CCETSW's Information Service in Belfast and obtain a copy of Information Sheet 17, address on p 109.

Qualifications and Awards

There are a number of nationally recognised qualifications and awards which automatically entitle holders to salary increments. Before you enrol on a course leading to a college award, especially one offered by a private college, for which you will have to pay, be sure to find out whether or not the award is recognised and, if it is, by whom. If you are thinking of studying at a private college that does not have a national reputation, it is a good idea to look into the examination success rate and present employment of its ex-students.

Additional Information

The information which follows was correct at the time of writing, but you should check it with the institution whose course you want to take or the examining body for whose award you wish to study, as changes occur all the time. When you write for a prospectus or for information, send a stamped and addressed envelope. You should also consult the following annual publications which can be found in most public libraries: *British Qualifications* (Kogan Page), CRAC *Directory of Further and Many Higher Education Courses in the UK* (Hobsons), CRAC *Degree Course Guides* (Hobsons), CRAC *Graduate Studies* (Hobsons), *Handbook of Degree and Advanced Courses* (Linneys ESL, Newgate Lane, Mansfield NG18 2PA).

Chapter 8
Courses, Qualifications and Awards

City and Guilds of London Institute (C&G)

C&G, Britain's largest testing and awarding body in technical and vocational education and training, offers a number of schemes leading to qualifications in caring. Courses are run in many colleges of further education throughout the UK.

Caring for Children 0–7 years (324)
Usually a part-time or in-service course for students aged 18 or over.

Family and Community Care (331)
Normally a two-year full-time course for 16- to 18-year-olds but may be shorter for mature students.

Practical Caring Skills (356)
A two-part scheme primarily for YT trainees in care placements.

Community Care Practice (325–1)
Usually a part-time or in-service course for students aged 18 and over.

Foundation Management for Care (325–2)
A scheme for those who hold or hope to take up a supervisory post in care.

Advanced Management for Care (325–3)
For senior staff and management in care.

Holders of certificates for the 331, 356 and 325–1 schemes work in a wide range of jobs with young and elderly people as well as people with special needs, in the public, private and voluntary sectors. An increasing number of people are progressing to further training after gaining work experience. Each of these schemes allows progression to Foundation and Advanced Management for Care (325–2/3). For further information including a list of centres offering courses, please contact C&G (see Useful Addresses).

Business and Technology Education Council (BTEC)

BTEC's awards are nationally recognised; courses are run in many colleges of further education throughout England and Wales.

First Certificate in Caring

First Diploma in Caring

National Diploma in Caring Services (Social Care)

For details and a list of centres offering courses, please contact BTEC (see Useful Addresses).

The Central Council for Education and Training in Social Work (CCTESW)

The CCETSW has statutory responsibility for promoting and recognising courses for training in all fields of social work, including residential and day services. At present there are three professional qualifications for social work: the Certificate of Qualification in Social Work (CQSW), the Certificate in Social Work (CSS) and the single qualifying award in social work, the Diploma in Social Work (DipSW) which is being phased in to replace the CQSW and which has already replaced the CSS. All three qualifications will continue to be recognised by the Council. The CCETSW also approves a number of preliminary and in-service courses – the Preliminary Course in Social Care (PCSC) and the In-Service Course in Social Care (ICSC) and the In-Service Course in Social Care (ICSC) but these will also be replaced in time by the all-embracing DipSW. Finally, Post-Qualifying Studies (PQS) are available to those wishing to take their professional development further, completing the full range of training opportunities on offer. The PQS does not lead to an award.

The CCETSW issues regularly updated leaflets connected with each of these awards and programmes and you are strongly advised to send for copies. When you do so, enclose a large (at least 15cm × 25cm) self-addressed envelope with a first class stamp affixed. You should also check details with the college in whose course you are interested.

The CCETSW and educational institutions would like to receive more applications from members of ethnic minority groups. If you apply to a course in the Clearing House (SWAS, page 111), you may include information about your ethnic background on the application form.

The Diploma in Social Work (DipSW)

The Diploma in Social Work has been developed to become the professional qualification for all social workers throughout the UK, wherever they work. It covers social workers in voluntary, statutory and private sectors; residential, day care, community education, health and probation. It has been designed to be flexible enough to meet the needs of all who wish to enter social work, at whatever stage in their career they are at.

The DipSW comprises at least two years of study and supervised practice. Candidates must be at least 21 and have two A levels to a satisfactory standard, and three other subjects at GCSE (Grades A–C), five passes at SCE including three Highers, or any other educational, professional or vocational qualification recognised as equivalent.

Courses leading to the DipSW were available at the following institutions at the time of writing this guide (1992). Many polytechnics are in the process of becoming universities:

Robert Gordon IT and Northern C, Aberdeen
Anglia HEC
University C, Bangor
Bath U
Queen's U, Belfast
Bourneville CFE, Birmingham and Birmingham U
Bradford U
Bristol Poly and U
Christ Church C and Kent University, Canterbury
Cheltenham and Gloucester CHE
Coventry Poly
Croydon C
Northern C, Dundee, and Dundee U
Durham U
Sevenson C and Lothian and Borders Consortium, Moray House C, Edinburgh
Exeter U
Jordanhill C, Queen's C, Langside CFE, Paisley CT, Glasgow, and Glasgow U
Huddersfield Poly
Hull U
Humberside Poly
Keele U
Leicester Poly and U

Kingston Poly, Middlesex Poly, Central London Poly, Royal Holloway and Bedford New C, London
Manchester U and Poly
Teeside Poly, Middlesbrough
Newcastle-upon-Tyne Poly
East Anglia U, Norwich
Nottingham Poly and U
Oxford Poly
South West Poly, Plymouth
Lancashire Poly, Preston
Sheffield City Poly and U
Southampton U
North Herts C, Stevenage
Stirling U
Stockport CF & HE
Staffordshire Poly, Stoke-on-Trent
Sunderland Poly
Sussex U
University C, Swansea
East Devon C, Tiverton
Ulster U
Bretton Hall, Wakefield
North Cheshire C, Warrington
Warwick U
North East Wales Institute, Wrexham

The Preliminary Certificate in Social Care (PCSC)

The PCSC is awarded by the CCETSW and, although it is not a professional qualification, most employers see it as evidence that the student is a suitable person to embark on a 'caring' career and some pay salary increments to PCSC holders. The two-year course leading to the PCSC is offered by colleges of further education throughout England, Wales and Northern Ireland. In Scotland preliminary training in social care is now under the auspices of SCOTVEC and you should write for information to the CCETSW's offices in Edinburgh (see p 109). No academic qualifications are required by CCETSW for entry to a PCSC course, but some colleges have their own entry requirements and most students hold some GCSE (or equivalent) passes. If your initial application is approved you will be interviewed.

The syllabus has been designed to give 16- to 19-year-olds a general background for a wide variety of caring work; they learn about social care institutions and provision for people with and without special needs. Students gain work experience in such places as nurseries and residential homes and while studying have the opportunity to continue their general education and take SCE and GSCE examinations. For further details send for CCETSW leaflets 6 and 6.1.

Colleges in England, Wales and Northern Ireland offering PCSC courses (check details with individual colleges)

Avon
Brunel TC

Bedfordshire
Barnfield C, Bedford CHE

Belfast
Belfast IFHE

Berkshire
Langley CFE, Newbury C

Buckinghamshire
Amersham CFEA&D, Milton Keynes C

Cambridgeshire
Isle C

Cheshire
Halton CFE, Macclesfield CFE, North Cheshire C, South Cheshire C, West Cheshire C

Cleveland
Kirby CFE

Clwyd
North Wales IHE

Cornwall
Cornwall CF&HE

Cumbria
Barrow-in-Furness CFE, Carlisle TC

Derbyshire
High Peak CFE, North-East Derbyshire CFE

Devon
East Devon CFE, Exeter C, Plymouth CFE

Dorset
Bournemouth and Poole CFE

County Down
North Down and Ards CFE, Newcastle CFE

Durham
New C Durham

Dyfed
Carmarthenshire CT

East Sussex
Lewes TC

Essex
Colchester I, Havering TC, Loughton CFE

Gloucestershire
Gloucestershire CAT

Greater London
Brixton C, City and East London
C, Enfield C, Erith CT, Haringey
C, Hounslow Borough C, C of
North West London, Waltham
Forest C

Greater Manchester
Bolton Metropolitan C, Bury
Metropolitan C, North
Manchester C, South Manchester
CC, Stockport CT, Tameside CT

Gwent
Newport CFE

Gwynedd
Gwynedd TC

Hampshire
Eastleigh CFE, Farnborough CT,
Highbury CT, The Tertiary C
Fareham

Hereford and Worcester
North Worcestershire C

Hertfordshire
Ware C

Humberside
East Yorkshire CFE, Hull CFE,
North Lindsey CT

Isle of Wight
Isle of Wight CAT

Kent
Thanet TC, West Kent CFE

Lancashire
Accrington and Rossendale C,
Blackpool and Fylde CF&HE,
Lancashire and Morecambe C,
Loughborough TC, Salford CT,
W R Tuson C, Wigan CT

Leicestershire
South Fields CFE

Lincolnshire
Grantham CFE

Londonderry
North West CT

Merseyside
Kirkby CFE, Sandown C,
Southport CAT, St Helen's C,
Wirral Metropolitan C

Mid Glamorgan
Bridgend CT

Norfolk
Norwich City CF&HE

North Yorkshire
Harrogate CAT, York CAT

Northamptonshire
Northampton CFE

Nottinghamshire
Arnold and Carlton C, Newark
TC

Oxfordshire
North Oxfordshire TC, Oxford
CFE

Powys
Radnor CFE

Shropshire
Telford CAT

Somerset
Somerset CAT

South Glamorgan
Barry CFE

South Yorkshire
Barnsley CT, Doncaster
Metropolitan I, Rotherham CAT,
Shirecliffe C

Staffordshire
Stoke on Trent C, Stafford CFE

Suffolk
Lowestoft C, Suffolk CF&HE

Surrey
Guildford CT

Tyne and Wear
Monkwearmouth CFE, North Tyneside CFE, South Tyneside C

County Tyrone
East Tyrone CFE

Warwickshire
Mid-Warwickshire CFE

West Glamorgan
Swansea C

West Midlands
Bilston CC, Bourneville CFE, Sutton Coldfield CFE, Tile Hill CFE

West Sussex
Crawley CT

West Yorkshire
Bradford and Ilkley CC, Huddersfield TC, Percival Whitley CFE, Thomas Danby C, Wakefield District C

Wiltshire
Trowbridge TC

The In-service Course in Social Care (ICSC)

The ICSC provides you with the chance to stand back from your work, see it in perspective and to learn from your own experience and that of your fellow students. No formal educational qualifications are required for this course but applicants (who do not have to be salaried staff) must be spending no fewer than two days per week providing social care, have had at least six months' experience in their present job and have received from their employer induction and basic job training. The course is intended for people working in local authority, voluntary or private homes and hostels, hospitals, special schools, sheltered housing, day centres, nurseries, foster care, domiciliary care and neighbourhood care and is complementary with induction and on-the-job training.

Coursework will reflect your on-the-job experience and examine the practice of different agencies serving a variety of client groups. You will learn about individual, family and social development, aspects of law and social policy, working relationships and the management of caring establishments. You will take part in discussion groups and make observation visits. Most courses last one day per week over three college terms and there are two three-day residential study periods. Your employer must grant you study leave, pay course fees and, normally, meet expenses for books, travel and subsistence, and will provide you with a study supervisor.

The CCETSW issues a Statement of Completion to each student who completes the work set by the tutor and attends not less than 80 per cent of the course. The Statement is not a qualification and is not dependent on formal assessment. However, with the help of your tutor and study supervisor you can evaluate what you have learned and how the course has helped you in your work. For further details send for CCETSW leaflets 5 and 5.1.

*Colleges Offering ICSC Courses
(check details with individual colleges)*

England

Avon
Brunel TC

Bedfordshire
Bedford CHE

Berkshire
Bracknell C

Buckinghamshire
Buckinghamshire CHE
Milton Keynes C

Cambridgeshire
Peterborough Regional C

Cheshire
North Cheshire C
South Cheshire C

Cleveland
Kirby CFE

Cornwall
Cornwall CF&HE

Cumbria
Barrow-in-Furness CFE
Carlisle TC
Kendal CFE
West Cumbria C

Derbyshire
Derbyshire CHE
High Peak C
North East Derbyshire CFE

Devon
East Devon CFE
North Devon C
Plymouth CFE
South Devon CAT

Dorset
Bournemouth and Poole CFE

Durham
Darlington CT
New C

Essex
Essex IHE
Colchester I
Loughton CFE

Gloucestershire
Gloucestershire CAT

Greater London
Bromley CT
City and East London C
Enfield C
Havering TC
Kilburn Poly
North London C
C of North West London
Southwark C
Waltham Forest C
West London IHE

Greater Manchester
North Manchester C
South Manchester CC
Salford CT
Stockport CT

Hampshire
Eastleigh CFE
Highbury CT
Southampton IHE

Hereford and Worcester
North Worcestershire C

Hertfordshire
Cassio C, Ware C

Humberside
East Yorkshire CFE
Grimsby CT
Humberside CHE
North Lindsey CT

Isle of Wight
Isle of Wight CAT

Kent
Canterbury CT
Mid Kent CH&FE
Thanet TC
West Kent CFE

Lancashire
Blackburn C
Blackpool and Fylde CF&HE
Bolton Metropolitan C
Burnley C
Lancashire and Morecambe CFE
W R Tuson C

Leicestershire
South Fields CFE

Lincolnshire
Grantham CFE
North Lincolnshire C

Merseyside
Sandown C
Southport CAT
Wirral Metropolitan C

Norfolk
Norwich City CF&HE

North Yorkshire
Harrogate CAT
York CT

Northamptonshire
Nene C

Northumberland
Northumberland CAT

Nottinghamshire
Basford Hall CFE
North Nottinghamshire CFE

Oxfordshire
Oxford CFE

Shropshire
Telford CAT

Somerset
Somerset CAT
Yeovil C

South Yorkshire
Barnsley CT
Rotherham CAT
Shirecliffe C

Staffordshire
Stafford CFE
Stoke-on-Trent C

Surrey
Guildford County CT
North East Surrey CT

Tyne and Wear
Hebburn Centre
Monkwearmouth CFE
Newcastle upon Tyne CAT
North Tyneside CFE

Warwickshire
North Warwickshire CTA

West Midlands
Bilston Community C
Bourneville C
Solihull CT
Sutton Coldfield CFE
Tile Hill CFE
Walsall CT

West Yorkshire
Bradford and Ilkley Community C
Huddersfield TC
Percival Whitley CFE
Thomas Danby C
Wakefield District C

Wiltshire
Trowbridge TC

Wales

Clwyd
North East Wales IHE

Dyfed
Carmarthenshire CTA

Gwent
Gwent CHE

Gwynedd
Gwynedd TC

Mid Glamorgan
Bridgend CT

South Glamorgan
South Glamorgan IHE

West Glamorgan
Swansea C

Scotland

Dumfries and Galloway
Dumfries and Galloway CT

Grampian
Robert Gordon's IT

Highland
Inverness CF&HE

Lothian
Moray House CE
Stevenson CFE

Strathclyde
Clydebank C
Craigie CE
Langside C
Motherwell C

Tayside
Northern CE

Western Isles
Lews Castle C

Northern Ireland

Belfast
Belfast Institute of FHE

County Down
North Down and Ards CFE

County Tyrone
East Tyrone CFE

The Certificate of Qualification in Social Work (CQSW)
The CQSW, to be replaced by the Diploma in Social Work, is the recognised professional qualification for social workers in day, field and residential services. CQSW courses and DipSW programmes vary in length and type and the course you choose will depend on your age, previous study and/or experience, on the availability of funding and on whether the course meets your needs in terms of locality, teaching methods and patterns, special areas of study and assessment methods. Although all courses and programmes lead to the qualification in social work, there is no nationally set syllabus. Students are expected to acquire knowledge and understanding of: social work theories, social policies, the local authority as an institution of government, the legal context of social work, human development; and theories of social change within a multicultural society. They learn how to assess situations requiring intervention, to plan intervention, to mobilise necessary resources and cooperate with others in their deployment, to use interviewing and group skills. They undertake periods of supervised practice in various social work settings in statutory and voluntary agencies. About half of all courses are taken up by practice placements. There are a number of different kinds of course and you should study Handbook 9.3 and individual college prospectuses. Information about financial aid during training and about how to apply for course places (procedures vary according to the course) is contained in the Handbook.

Courses for Graduates
These are normally open to holders of a degree from a UK university or

from the CNAA or an overseas equivalent. One-year CQSW courses are
for those holding a relevant social science degree, diploma or certificate.
Two-year CQSW and DipSW programmes are for those who hold non-
relevant degrees and have pre-course experience.

Institutions offering one-year graduate courses
(the last intake is 1992)

Croydon C	Manchester C
Leeds Poly	University of North Wales,
Goldsmith C	Bangor

Institutions offering two-year graduate courses

Aberdeen U	Liverpool Poly
Queen's U, Belfast	London S of Economics
Birmingham U	South Bank Poly
Bristol U	Manchester U
Cardiff U	Middlesex Poly
Cheltenham and Gloucester CHE	Nottingham U
Christchurch C, Canterbury	Oxford Poly
Dundee U	Oxford U
Durham U	Robert Gordon's IT, Aberdeen
U of East Anglia	Sheffield U
Edinburgh U	Southampton U
Royal Holloway and Bedford New	Stirling U
C	Sussex U
Exeter U	Ulster U, Magee
Glasgow U	University C, Swansea
Hull U	University of North Wales,
Keele U	Bangor
Kent U	Warwick U
Lancaster U	York U
Leicester U	

Courses for Undergraduates

Some institutions of higher education offer four-year degree courses
recognised by the CCETSW as leading to the CQSW or the DipSW. The
degree is usually in social science combined with different options, one
of which leads to the professional social work qualification. You need to
satisfy degree-course entry requirements for these courses.

Institutions offering four-year degree courses

Bath U	Glasgow U
Birmingham Poly	Hatfield Poly
Birmingham U	Lancashire Poly
Bradford U	Lancaster U
Buckinghamshire CHE	Middlesex Poly
Coventry Poly	Newcastle upon Tyne Poly

North East London Poly
North London Poly
Nottingham Poly
Paisley CT
Plymouth Poly
Robert Gordon's IT, Aberdeen

Sheffield City Poly
Southampton U
Stirling U
Ulster U, Coleraine/
Jordanstown/Magee

Two-year Courses for Non-graduates

The minimum age for starting is normally 20, but most successful applicants are older. Some institutions will not accept applicants over the age of 50. Candidates for CQSW aged 20 to 24 must normally hold at least five GCSEs at Grade A, B or C (or equivalent) including English or Welsh, and many colleges require A levels (or equivalent). Candidates aged 25 and over for CQSW, or 21 and over for DipSW, are not required to have formal educational qualifications but should be able to provide evidence of ability to study at an advanced level and have relevant paid or voluntary work experience. Mature students (aged 30 and over) are welcomed by some institutions, which may give priority to applicants looking to social work as a change of career. Previous social work experience may not be required.

Institutions offering two-year non-graduate courses

Aberdeen U
Birmingham Poly
Brentwood IHE
Bristol Poly
Bristol U
Buckinghamshire CHE
Bulmershe CHE, Reading
Cardiff U
Central London Poly
Christchurch C, Canterbury
Cheltenham and Gloucester CHE
Coventry Poly
Croydon C
East Devon C, Tiverton
Huddersfield Poly
Humberside Poly
Jordanhill CE
Kingston Poly
Lancashire Poly
Leeds Poly
Leicester Poly
Liverpool Poly
Liverpool U
Manchester Poly
Manchester U
Mid-Kent CF&HE

Middlesex Poly
Moray House CE, Edinburgh
Nene C, Northampton
Newcastle upon Tyne Poly
North East London Poly
North East Wales IHE, Wrexham
North London Poly
Northern CE, Dundee
Nottingham Poly
Oxford Poly
Plymouth Poly
Portsmouth Poly
Robert Gordon's IT, Aberdeen
Ruskin C, Oxford
Selly Oak C, Birmingham
Sheffield City Poly
South Glamorgan IHE
Southampton U
Stevenage C
Stirling U
Suffolk CH&FE, Ipswich
Sunderland Poly
Teesside Poly
Ulster U, Jordanstown
West London IHE

Courses for People with Family Commitments

A few extended courses are provided for those whose family commitments prevent their taking the regular courses. The course content is the same as on the other CQSW courses but the college day and practice placements are shorter and there may be longer holidays.

Institutions offering extended or sandwich courses

Croydon C (3-y non-grad)
Queen's C, Glasgow (3-y non-grad)
Huddersfield Poly (3-y part-time)
Liverpool Poly (3-y non-grad)
Newcastle upon Tyne Poly (3-y non-grad)
Stevenage C (3-y non-grad)
Warwick U (2-y grad)

How to Apply

Applications for a place on a postgraduate or non-graduate CQSW course should be made through the Social Work Admissions System (SWAS), Fulton House, Jessop Avenue, Cheltenham, Gloucestershire GL50 3SH.

Post-qualifying Studies (PQS)

The CCETSW promotes and approves a number of PQS programmes. These focus on advanced practice or on preparation for new roles, such as management, supervision or research. They are designed to give students the opportunity to undertake substantial periods of study and normally contain a practice element. Minimum length: one full term or its equivalent in part-time study (ie 60 days). PQS programmes are not intended to convert qualifications, eg from residential to field-work, or as a substitute for professional or other qualifications.

No award is made by the CCETSW to students successfully completing a PQS programme, but their names are entered on a register. Students are normally seconded to a CCETSW-approved PQS course by their employer. For those who have not been seconded, the source of a grant will depend on the type of programme (eg full or part time) and on which part of the UK they live and intend to work in. Entry requirements: CQSW, SCRCCYP, CRSW, CRCCYP, DTMHA or equivalent qualifications issued by CCETSW's predecessors, plus two years' practical experience since qualifying (more experience may be necessary for many types of study). For full details send for CCETSW leaflet 8.

The Programmes

PQS/3 Advanced Interdisciplinary Training in Family Therapy combined with MSc awarded by Brunel U.

PQS/4 One-year Advanced Programme for Social Workers. Tavistock Clinic.

PQS/6 MSc (Econ) in Applied Social Studies: Options in Social Work Education, Social Work Management and Administration, and Residential Social Work. UC Cardiff.

PQS/7 MA in Public and Social Administration: Options in Personal Social Services, Policy and Organisation, and in Social Security. Brunel U.

PQS/12 Continuing Education Programme: Course in Social Work Education: A Programme in Learning and Change. National Institute for Social Work, London.

PQS/16 MA in Social and Community Work. Bradford U.

PQS/23 Ageing, Health and Social Care. Southampton U.

PQS/24 Personal Social Service Fellowships. Bristol U.

PQS/25 Post-qualifying Course in Social Work in Mental Health Settings by part-time study. Maudsley and Bethlem Royal Hospital, Southwark Social Services Department, London U.

PQS/26 Supervision and Management in Social Work. Sussex U.

PQS/31 MA/Dip in Social Service Planning. Essex U.

PQS/33 MSc/Diploma in Psychiatric Social Work. Manchester U.

PQS/34 MSc/Diploma in Policy Analysis and Development. Bath U.

PQS/36 Post-qualifying Course in Family Therapy. Newcastle upon Tyne Poly.

PQS/38 Diploma in Alcohol Studies. Paisley CT.

PQS/39 Post-qualifying Programme of Individual Study for Experienced Social Workers. Edinburgh U.

PQS/43 Day Care and Work with Families of Young Children. Bristol U.

PQS/44 MSc Research Programme in Social Policy and Institutions. Cranfield IT.

PQS/48 Post-qualifying Course in Social Work Education. Jordanhill CE.

PQS/51 MSc in Social Research Methods with Option in Social Services and Social Work Research. Surrey U.

PQS/52 MSc (Social Research) with Option in Social Services and Social Work Research. Surrey U.

PQS/54 Postgraduate Certificate in the Practice of Social Welfare in Mental Health. Surrey U.

PQS/55 Personal Research Programme. Southampton U.

PQS/56 Social Work, People and Disability. Manchester U.

PQS/57 Diploma in Advanced Social Work (Children and Families). Goldsmiths' C in association with British Agencies for Adoption and Fostering.

PQS/58 MSc in Advanced Social Work Studies. Edinburgh U.

PQS/59 Diploma in Advanced Social Work Studies. Exeter U.

PQS/60 Certificate in Social Work Management. Liverpool Poly.

PQS/61 Master's Degree in Social Work Studies. U of East Anglia.

PQS/62 Post-qualifying Course in Child Care Practice, Policy and Research linked to registration for an MPhil or PhD. Tavistock Clinic and NE London Poly.

PQS/64 MSc in Public Sector Management (Social and Community Services Option). Aston U.

PQS/65 Training Programme in Family Therapy. Scottish I of Human Relations, Edinburgh.

PQS/66 Family Therapy Training (Parts I and II). I of Family Therapy, London.

PQS/67 Diploma/MSc in Mental Health, Southampton U.

PQS/68 Diploma in Social Learning Theory and Practice in Applied Settings. Leicester U.

PQS/69 Working Together with People with a Mental Handicap: The Team Approach. South Glamorgan IHE.

PQS/70 Working Together with People with a Mental Handicap: The Team Approach. Carmarthenshire CTA.

PQS/73 Master's Degree in Social Science (Social Services Management) and Diploma in Social Services Management. Birmingham U.

PQS/74 Advanced Certificate in Social Work with Young Offenders. West Sussex IHE.

PQS/75 Development in Mental Handicap Work. Bedfordshire S of Nursing and Bedfordshire Social Services Department.

PQS/76 Advanced Social Work (Child Protection). Dundee U.

PQS/77 The North West Region's Post-qualifying Course in Child Protection. Lancaster U.

PQS/78 Advanced Social Work Studies: MPhil in Social Work. Brunel U and Tavistock Clinic.

PQS/79 Behavioural Approaches for Professionals Working with People who have Learning Difficulties. Hester Adrian Research Centre, Manchester U.

PQS/80 Diploma in Family Therapy. Manchester U.

PQS/81 Developing and Managing Services for People with Learning Difficulties. Consortium from North London, Western Regional Health

Authority, Association of Directors of Social Services (North West Branch), Manchester U, Health Services Management Unit.

PQS/82 MA/Diploma in Child Care Law and Practice. Keele U.

Youth and Community Work

The Youth Service is a partnership between central government, local education authorities and voluntary organisations. The Council for Education and Training in Youth and Community Work is concerned with all aspects of initial and in-service training and educational needs for full-time youth and community workers. It produces a useful booklet, *Initial Training Courses in Youth and Community Work*. The National Youth Bureau provides training and research services in the youth services field.

Professional Qualifications

A youth worker or community centre warden is considered qualified only if he/she satisfies one of the following criteria. He/she:

(a) has satisfactorily completed a two-year full-time certificate/ diploma course of initial training for youth workers and/or community centre wardens held at or sponsored by the following institutions:

England
Bradford and Ilkley C, Bulmershe CHE (Reading), Crewe and Alsager CHE, Derbyshire CHE, Durham U, Goldsmiths C (London), Leeds Poly, Leicester Poly, Manchester Poly, Matlock C of Ed, National Council of YMCAs in association with NE London Poly, Sunderland Poly, Westhill C of Ed (Birmingham)

Wales
NE Wales Institute

Northern Ireland
U of Ulster;

or (b) has satisfactorily completed a one-year postgraduate training course for youth workers and/or community centre wardens held at: Aberdeen C of Ed, Dundee C of Ed, Westhill C of Ed (Birmingham);

or (c) has satisfactorily completed a part-time course of training at Thames Poly, Manchester Poly, YMCA/Poly of East London (distance learning), Turning Point (apprenticeship scheme) or U of Ulster;

or (d) is a fully qualified teacher, meeting the requirements of the Secretary of State for Education and Science. This applies only to those who qualified before 1988, after which date the only teaching qualification recognised will be the BEd (Youth Work) degrees of Roehampton I, Westhill C, Crewe and Alsager CHE, St Martin's C (Lancaster), Avery Hill C (London);

or (e) holds a UK university or CNAA diploma or degree of a social science faculty, or other such qualification as the Committee and Secretary of State for Education and Science may approve, and can produce evidence that the course of study included appropriate youth and/or community content and a period of supervised relevant practical work. Applications are considered individually by the Joint Negotiating Committee;

or (f) holds one of the following degrees: U of Ulster BA (Hons) Youth and Community Work, Brunel U BSc (Combined Hons) or Bradford and Ilkley C BA (Hons) Community Studies.

Youth and Community Work in Scotland

The importance of youth and community work has long been acknowledged in Scotland, where it is generally known as community education. Training courses are run at three colleges of education, and although the content of the courses is broadly in line with courses in the rest of the British Isles, other arrangements are a little different. Students are accepted from the age of 18 for three-year courses and from the age of 23, with working experience, for two-year courses. The academic qualifications required are: for 18- to 22-year-olds, four Highers, or three Highers and two O grades, or two Highers and four O grades; for older entrants, three Highers, or two Highers and two O grades. Grants are obtained, not from the local authority, but from the Scottish Education Department Awards Branch, Haymarket House, Clifton Terrace, Edinburgh EH12 5DT. Applications should be made to the individual colleges.

Colleges Running Courses Leading to the Diploma in Community Education
Dundee C of Ed, Jordanhill C of Ed, Moray House C of Ed

Note: Graduates and holders of certain professional qualifications can take a one-year course leading to the award of the Certificate in Youth and Community Service at the above colleges.

All general enquiries about careers in community education should be addressed to: The Scottish Community Education Council.

University Awards

Birmingham U Certificate in Youth and Community Work: Westhill C; Diploma in Community Work: Westhill C; Lancaster U Postgraduate Certificate in Youth Work; St Martin's C; Nottingham U Certificate in Youth and Community Studies: Derbyshire CHE.

Polytechnic Awards

Leicester Poly CNAA Certificate in Youth and Community Development; Manchester Poly, CNAA Certificate in Youth and Community Work; Sunderland Poly Certificate in Community and Youth Work.

Other Awards

Regional award
Certificate in Youth and Community Work: Rotherham CAT.

College awards
Diploma in Youth and Community Work/Studies: Manchester Poly, Plater C Oxford, Ulster U, Jordanhill CE, Thames Poly, North East Wales IHE
Diploma in Community Education (Youth and Community): Moray House CE
Certificate in Youth and Community Leadership: Rupert Stanley CFE.

The Youth Development Trust

The YDT (see Useful Addresses) has several degrees of membership – Fellowship, Membership, Associateship, Affiliateship – and conducts an examination for its Diploma of Youth Development. The YDT has standing liaison arrangements with other bodies in the Youth Work, Play Work, Social Welfare, Leisure and Education fields as a policy of cross-boundary support and training.

Health Visiting

To work as a health visitor it is necessary to have completed a professional course approved by the UK Central Council for Nursing, Midwifery and Health Visiting (see address on p 111). You need tact, initiative and the ability to communicate with people at all levels. There are six types of courses available:

> Post-RGN courses for which you must be a Registered General Nurse and have at least five GCSEs (A–C) or their equivalent or have passed an entrance exam approved by the UKCC;
> Modified courses for graduates;
> Degree courses with a health visiting option;
> Integrated degree courses leading to a nursing and health visitor qualification and a relevant degree;
> Post-graduate diploma courses;
> Extended courses for RGNs who wish to study part-time over a two-year period.

Courses last at least 51 weeks and include a study of human growth and development and its application to the principles and practice of health visiting.

Overleaf is a selection of training centres currently offering courses. Write to the UKCC or the Health Visitors' Association (see address on p 110) for a full list.

1. Post-registration Courses

Birmingham
Birmingham Poly

Brighton
Brighton Poly

Bristol
Bristol Poly

Cardiff
Welsh National School of
Medicine

Coventry
Coventry Poly

Durham
School of Post Experience
Studies

Hull
University of Hull

Leeds
Leeds Poly

Leicester
Leicester Poly

Liverpool
University of Liverpool

London
Polytechnic of East London
Polytechnic of North London

Manchester
Manchester Poly

Oxford
Oxford Poly

Reading
University of Reading

Swansea
University College of Swansea

2. Modified Courses for Graduates
Available at many of the colleges to graduates of relevant disciplines.

3. Post-RGN Courses with HV Option

London
Polytechnic of East London

4. RGN Integrated Degree Courses with HV Option

Liverpool
University of Liverpool

London
King's College, University of
London

Southampton
University of Southampton

5. Postgraduate Diploma in Health Visiting

London
South Bank Poly

6. Extended Courses

Hatfield
Hatfield Poly

Preston
Lancashire Poly

Scotland

Students seeking information about courses in Scotland should contact the National Board for Nursing, Midwifery and Health Visiting for Scotland. (See address on p 110.)

Occupational Therapy

State registration is necessary for employment as an occupational therapist, and training takes from two to four years depending on your academic qualifications. Full-time three/four year courses leading to the BSc in Occupational Therapy are available at a number of institutions of higher education, and in-service and accelerated courses leading to the Diploma of the College of Occupational Therapists (DipCOT) are offered at some private schools, colleges and health authority departments. The minimum age for entry is 18 years ($17\frac{1}{2}$ in Scotland) and you must have five GCSE passes (grades A–C), including two at A level. At least one subject must be science, and biology is particularly useful. Certain schools will take alternative qualifications, such as the BTEC National Diploma. Graduates with relevant degrees can take two-year accelerated courses. Other ways to qualify include having worked as a Helper or Technical Instructor for at least a year, or if you are a mature candidate with evidence of a broad, general education.

Courses include the study of anatomy, physiology, psychology, sociology, medical and surgical conditions, orthopaedics, psychiatry, techniques and skills used in OT, administration and management. Nearly one-third of the courses is spent in practical work.

The College of Occupational Therapists is setting up a clearing house to handle applications for training places and you should write to the Occupational Therapy Training Clearing House (address on p 110) for its 'Handbook for Candidates' which at the time of writing was in preparation. The Clearing House system is unlikely to be in operation until 1993, so until then apply as shown on the list below, through: PCAS, PO Box 67, Cheltenham, Gloucestershire GL50 3AP; or UCCA, PO Box 28, Cheltenham, Gloucestershire GL50 1HY; or directly to the school. Applications should be made by the end of September in the year before the one in which you wish to start your training.

Aberdeen
The Grampian School of Occupational Therapy, Woolmanhill, Aberdeen AB9 1QS (Direct)

Canterbury
Canterbury Christ Church College, North Holmes Road, Canterbury, Kent CT1 1QU (PCAS)

Cardiff
The Welsh School of Occupational Therapy, Combined Training Institute, University Hospital of Wales, Heath Park, Cardiff CF4 4XW (Direct)

Coventry
West Midland Regional School of Occupational Therapy, Coventry Polytechnic, Priory Street, Coventry CV1 5FB (PCAS)

Derby
The Derby School of Occupational Therapy, Whitaker Road, Derby DE3 6AP (PCAS)

Edinburgh
The Department of Occupational Therapy, Queen Margaret College, Clerwood Terrace, Edinburgh EH12 8TS (Direct)

Essex
Essex School of Occupational Therapy, Middlesex Health Authority, Collingwood Road, Witham, Essex CM8 2TT (Direct)

Exeter
St Loye's School of Occupational Therapy, Millbrook House, Millbrook Lane, Topsham Road, Exeter EX2 6ES (UCCA)

Glasgow
Glasgow School of Occupational Therapy, The Queen's College, Southbrae Drive, Glasgow G13 1PP (Direct)

Liverpool
Department of Occupational Therapy, St Katherine's College, Liverpool Institute of Higher Education, Stand Park Road, PO Box 6, Liverpool L16 9JD (UCCA)

London
The London School of Occupational Therapy, West London Institute of Higher Education, Borough Road, Isleworth TW7 5DU (PCAS)

School of Occupational Therapy, The London Hospital Medical College, 40 New Road, London E1 2AX (Direct)

Newcastle
Department of Health and Behavioural Studies, Newcastle upon Tyne Polytechnic, Coach Lane Campus, Coach Lane, Newcastle upon Tyne NE7 7XA (PCAS)

Northampton
School of Occupational Therapy, St Andrew's Hospital, Northampton NN1 5DG (Direct)

Northern Ireland
Department of Occupational Therapy and Physiotherapy, Faculty of Social and Health Sciences, University of Ulster, Jordanstown Campus, Newtownabbey, Co Antrim BT37 0QB (UCCA)

Oxford
Dorset House School of Occupational Therapy, 58 London Road, Headington, Oxford OX3 7PE (PCAS)

Salford
The School of Occupational Therapy, Salford College of Technology, Frederick Road, Salford, Lancashire M6 6PU (PCAS)

York
Department of Occupational Therapy, College of Ripon and York St John, Lord Mayor's Walk, York YO3 7EX (UCCA)

Counselling

The professional accrediting agency is the British Association for Counselling (BAC), which will tell you how to obtain accreditation and will supply information on training and careers. The only courses recognised and recommended by BAC under the Courses Recognition Scheme of 1988 are those given below. Other courses may meet the criteria laid down by BAC but cannot be recommended as at the time of writing this guide they have not been through the accreditation procedure.

Higher Degrees Awarded by Universities
Durham: MA Guidance & Counselling
East Anglia: MA Pastoral Care & Guidance
Glasgow: MAppSci Educational Psychology & Child Guidance
Hull: MA Personal, Social & Moral Education
Nottingham: MEd Human Relations
Reading: MA Counselling & Guidance
Sheffield: MA Art & Psychotherapy
Strathclyde: MSc in Careers Guidance & Employment Counselling
Ulster: MSc Guidance & Counselling
Warwick: MSc Psychotherapy

Diplomas Awarded by Universities
Birmingham: Pastoral Studies
Keele: Counselling Studies
Kent: Alcohol Counselling & Consultation
Leeds: Education & Further Education (Collegiate) Guidance & Counselling
Liverpool: Guidance & Careers Education
London: *Institute of Education* Pastoral Care, Counselling & Welfare in Education
London: *Extra-Mural Studies Dept* Student Counselling
Manchester: Advanced Study in Guidance & Counselling in Education
North Wales, University College: Counselling
Nottingham: Counselling Skills for Pastoral Care; Education (Counselling)
Reading: Postgraduate Diploma Counselling & Guidance
Strathclyde: Postgraduate Diploma Careers Guidance

Ulster: Postgraduate Diploma Guidance & Counselling; Careers Guidance
Wales: *Cardiff* Pastoral Studies

Diplomas Awarded by Polytechnics
Birmingham: Polytechnic Diploma Careers Guidance
Brighton: Polytechnic Diploma Counselling
Bristol: Postgraduate Diploma Careers Guidance (LGTB)
Hatfield: Polytechnic Diploma Counselling
North East London: Diploma Guidance & Counselling (Education & Community Health)
Manchester: Polytechnic Diploma Counselling
Sheffield: Diploma Guidance in Schools

Certificates Awarded by Universities
Edinburgh: Pastoral Studies
Exeter: Certificate Counselling
London: *Extra-Mural Studies Dept* Extra-Mural Certificate Student Counselling
Reading: Postgraduate Certificate Vocational Guidance

Other Courses
Salvation Army: The Social Services Section of the Salvation Army holds recognised 2-year day-release courses in Pastoral Counselling

Diploma Courses Recognised by BAC
Bristol: University of Bristol, Dept for Continuing Education, Wills Memorial Building, Queen's Road, Bristol B58 1HR – Diploma in Counselling
Cleveland: Stockton Psychotherapy Training Institute, 77 Acklam Road, Thornaby-on-Tees, Cleveland TS17 7BD – Diploma in Humanistic Counselling
Colchester: Colchester Institute, Sheepen Road, Colchester, Essex CO3 3LL – Diploma in Counselling
Glasgow: Person Centred Therapy, c/o Dave Mearns, Psychology Dept, Jordanhill College, Glasgow G13 1PP – Person Centred Approach to Counselling and Psychotherapy
London: Centre for Counselling and Psychotherapy Education, 21 Lancaster Road, London W11 1QL – Diploma in Counselling and Psychotherapy

Metanoia, 13 North Common Road, London W5 2QB – Diploma in Person Centred Counselling

Polytechnic of East London, Romford Road, London E15 4LZ – Diploma in Counselling and Guidance

Psychosynthesis and Education Trust, 92/94 Tooley Street, London SE1 2TH – Counsellors' Diploma (Professional Training Programme)

Westminster Pastoral Foundation, 23 Kensington Square, London W8
5HN - Diploma in Advanced Psychodynamic Counselling
Manchester: South Manchester College, Arden Centre, Sale Road
Northenden, Manchester M23 0DD - Manchester Counselling Course
Diploma
Wigan: Wigan College of Technology, Dept of Social Science, Parsons
Walk, Wigan WN1 1RR - Advanced Diploma in Counselling and
Advanced Certificate in Counselling

Marriage Guidance Counselling (Relate)

The training is a two-year workshop programme based on three
modular structures. Each module is made up of two 48-hour residential
courses at Herbert Gray College, Rugby, and a regional component.
Teaching strategies include formal presentation by tutors, informal
seminars and small discussion groups, case studies, counselling skills
and exercises, role play, use of audio-visual material and equipment,
and guided reading. Instead of examinations there is continuous
assessment spread over the entire training period and trainees are
encouraged to take an active part in their own assessment.

Trainees who have successfully completed the basic counsellor
training, have submitted a 3,000-word casework project to the required
standard, and have carried out 400 hours of counselling, are awarded
the Certificate of Marital and Couple Counselling.

A Diploma in Marital and Couple Counselling is currently being
developed and the training should be available from 1993.

Marital Sexual Therapy
Only trained marriage guidance counsellors are accepted for the
course, which lasts 16 months and consists of five short residential
sessions at Rugby and regional training. Both trainee MSTs and trained
therapists attend regular case discussion groups, update their knowledge and have private tutorials three times a year with a suitably
qualified person. Further details can be obtained from your local Relate
centre, which will be listed in the telephone directory, or from Herbert
Gray College (address on p 110).

Chapter 9
Recommended Reading

Where to Look for Jobs

Community Care
Daily Mail (local government posts on Wednesdays)
The Guardian (Tuesdays and Wednesdays)
New Statesman & Society
Scan (from Scottish Community Education Centre)
Scope (from Council of Social Service for Northern Ireland)
Social Work Today
The Times Educational Supplement (a few jobs within the education service)
Young People Now (from National Youth Bureau)

If you are making your own general enquiries you will find the names of authorities and organisations to whom you can write in the *Education Yearbook, Social Services Yearbook* and *Voluntary Agencies Directory*.

The Scottish Community Education Council runs a clearing house for youth posts in Scotland.

The Community and Youth Workers Union keeps information on vacant posts in England and Wales. You should state what part of the country you wish to work in when you enquire.

Background Reading

Introducing Social Work CCETSW leaflet 1.4

There are too many book titles to list individually; you can pursue the subjects that interest you by sending for the publications lists of: The British Association for Counselling, the British Association of Social Workers, MIND, the National Council for Voluntary Organisations and the Scottish Council for Community and Voluntary Organisations. (See Chapter 10 for addresses.)

Chapter 10
Useful Addresses

British Association for Counselling, 1 Regent Place, Rugby, Warwickshire CV21 2PJ

British Association of Art Therapists, 11a Richmond Road, Brighton, East Sussex BN2 3RL

British Association of Social Workers, 16 Kent Street, Birmingham B5 6RD

British Society for Music Therapy, 69 Avondale Avenue, East Barnet, Hertfordshire EN4 8NB

BTEC Information Office, Central House, Upper Woburn Place, London WC1H 0HH

CCETSW Information Service, Derbyshire House, St Chad's Street, London WC1H 8AD; *or* 9 South David Street, Edinburgh EH2 2BW; *or* West Wing, St David's House, Wood Street, Cardiff CF1 1ES; *or* 14 Malone Road, Belfast BT9 5BN

Central Council for Education and Training in Social Work see CCETSW

Citizens' Advice Bureaux (consult local telephone directory)

City and Guilds of London Institute, 46 Britannia Street, London WC1X 9RG

Civil Service Commission, Alencon Link, Basingstoke, Hampshire RG21 1JB

College of Occupational Therapists, 6–8 Marshalsea Road, London SE1 1HL

College of Speech and Language Therapists, Harold Poster House, 6 Lechmere Road, London NW2 5BH

Community Service Volunteers, 237 Pentonville Road, London N1 9JN; *or* 22 High Street, Belfast BT1 2BD; *or* 236 Clyde Street, Glasgow

Council of Social Service for Northern Ireland, 2 Annandale Avenue, Belfast BT7 3JH

Department of Social Security, Alexander Fleming House, Elephant and Castle, London SE1 6TE

English National Board for Nursing, Midwifery and Health Visiting, Victory House, 170 Tottenham Court Road, London W1P 0HA

Health Visitors' Association, 50 Southwark Street, London SE1 1UN

Herbert Gray College, Little Church Street, Rugby, Warwickshire CV21 3AP

Home Office (HM Prison Service), Room 403, Cleland House, Page Street, London SW1P 4LN

Home Office (Probation Service Division), Queen Anne's Gate, London SW1H 9AT

MIND, National Association for Mental Health, 22 Harley Street, London W1N 2ED

NACRO, 169 Clapham Road, London SW9 0PU

National Association of Probation Officers, 3-4 Chivalry Road, London SW11 1HT

National Board for Nursing, Midwifery and Health Visiting for Northern Ireland, RAC House, 79 Chichester Street, Belfast BT1 4JE

National Board for Nursing, Midwifery and Health Visiting for Scotland, 22 Queen Street, Edinburgh EH2 1JX

National Council for Voluntary Organisations, 26 Bedford Square, London WC1B 3HU

National Council for Voluntary Youth Services, Wellington House, 29 Albion Street, Leicester LE1 6GD

National Union of Students, Nelson Mandela House, 461 Holloway Road, London N7 6LJ

National Youth Agency, 17-23 Albion Street, Leicester LE1 6GO

Occupational Therapy Training Clearing House, The College of Occupational Therapists, 6-8 Marshalsea Road, London SE1 1HL

Polytechnics Central Admissions System (PCAS), PO Box 67, Cheltenham, Gloucestershire GL50 3AP

Relate: National Marriage Guidance (previously Marriage Guidance Council; consult local telephone directory)

SACRO, 53 George Street, Edinburgh EH2 2ET

Samaritans (consult local telephone directory)

Scottish Community Education Council, West Coates House, 90 Haymarket Terrace, Edinburgh EH12 5LQ

Scottish Council for Community and Voluntary Organisations, 18-19 Claremont Crescent, Edinburgh EH7 4QD

Scottish Marriage Guidance Council, 26 Frederick Street, Edinburgh EH2 2JR

Scottish Prison Service, St Margaret's House, 151 London Road, Edinburgh EH8 7TQ

Social Work Admissions System (SWAS), Fulton House, Jessop Avenue, Cheltenham, Gloucestershire GL50 3SH

Soldiers', Sailors' and Airmen's Families Association, 19 Queen Elizabeth Street, London SE1 2LP

UK Central Council for Nursing, Midwifery and Health Visiting, 23 Portland Place, London W1N 3AF

Universities Central Council on Admissions (UCCA), PO Box 28, Cheltenham, Gloucestershire GL50 1HY

Volunteer Centre, 29 Lower King's Road, Berkhamsted, Hertfordshire HP4 2AB

Wales Council for Voluntary Action, Llys Ifor, Crescent Road, Caerphilly, Mid Glamorgan CF8 1XL

Welsh National Board for Nursing, Midwifery and Health Visiting, Floor 13, Pearl Assurance House, Greyfriars Road, Cardiff CF1 3AG

Youth Development Trust, Elliot House, Jackson Row, Manchester M2